T0156716

Also by Robert Roselli "The THEorY of LIVEvolution: "Great" Society of the UN-Dead" available on www.boxofsunglasses.com

THE UN-AMERICAN GENOCIDAL COMPLEX

ROBERT ROSELLI

iUniverse, Inc.
New York   Bloomington

The UN-American Genocidal Complex

Copyright © 2010 Robert Roselli

All rights reserved. No part of this book may be used or reproduced by any means, graphic, electronic, or mechanical, including photocopying, recording, taping or by any information storage retrieval system without the written permission of the publisher except in the case of brief quotations embodied in critical articles and reviews.

iUniverse books may be ordered through booksellers or by contacting:

iUniverse
1663 Liberty Drive
Bloomington, IN 47403
www.iuniverse.com
1-800-Authors (1-800-288-4677)

Because of the dynamic nature of the Internet, any Web addresses or links contained in this book may have changed since publication and may no longer be valid. The views expressed in this work are solely those of the author and do not necessarily reflect the views of the publisher, and the publisher hereby disclaims any responsibility for them.

ISBN: 978-1-4502-3547-1 (pbk)
ISBN: 978-1-4502-3548-8 (ebook)

Printed in the United States of America

iUniverse rev. date: 7/1/10

This book is dedicated to two groups. The first is comprised of those who have given their lives in the protection of this once Godly nation against all enemies without. This encompasses General and President George Washington, the greatest American that ever lived, to the faceless private who never made it home from Iwo Jima . On the flip side, it is dedicated to "Them" and their predecessors. Today "They" are the Rockefeller-Kissinger-Brzezinski-Soros led UN-American Genocidal Complex and their enigmatic sun of god "President" Barack Obama who have taken it from within thereby negating the Divine and selfless efforts of the first group. Congratulations to you worshippers of Baal, modern day money-changers, Communist sellouts and "cosmic messengers" on the accomplishment of your "Great" Plan for your "Great" Society. You've won.

And the best of luck with "Mother Russia", Red China and "the religion of peace" not to mention your upcoming trial before the "Supreme Judge of the world"; you're going to need it.

Front Cover: 3 key elements of the "UN-American Genocidal Complex": The Georgia Guidestones, "Skull and Bones" logo of "The Order" and the UN-dead Building, New York City.

Pleased to meet you, hope you guess my name...

Contents

Preface

This book, my second, will hopefully shock the "average" reader in to the realization of the evil "They" are capable of; an evil that can only be ascribed to "The Angel of Light" or "the serpent" himself. As someone who has read copious sources as diverse as the King James Bible to "New" Age guru Helena Blavatsky and the "Ascended Master" Djwhal Khul who "spoke" through Lucius Trust (a current NGO or non-governmental organization of the United Nations) founder Alice Bailey I can tell you that when one peels away the onion layers of "the conspiracy" you end up back at the Garden of Eden. Have no doubt that "They" have one goal in mind: the elimination of a large portion of the world's population and outright socio-economic control of what "They" allow to remain since "They" have already anointed themselves as "God". So whether it's the establishment of genocidal maniacs like Adolf Hitler, the horrific "science" of evolution and today's radical environmental movement, the blatant scam of the "Federal" "Reserve" system or the purposeful deployment of killer diseases like AIDS all is designed to achieve those two ends. For more background please visit my web site www.boxofsunglasses.com to investigate these things and more to your own satisfaction. Everything that I say or write is corroborated with ample footnotes and bibliographical information. Please check out some of them for yourself before passing judgment. Both in this book and on the web site I strive to provide the correct balance between establishing enough background versus length in terms of the time invested in reading the information. Unfortunately there's more; much more to "the conspiracy". As much as I have read and subsequently written it only represents the tip of the iceberg. But maybe this is enough as the tip warns of the much bigger danger lurking beneath.

List of Illustrations

*Replaced with text due to trademark issues.

Introduction

The "UN-American Genocidal Complex" is an obvious derivation from the "military-industrial complex" that former Oval Office Occupier, World War II General and might I say "conspiracy theorist" Dwight Eisenhower warned about on his way out the door after his tenure as the one responsible for keeping the seat in the Oval Office warm. As you'll learn by the end of this book the "military-industrial complex" and "The UN-American Genocidal Complex" are essentially the same circles of power inside these "Late Great United States" and are in fact those responsible for making this once great nation just that, "The Late Great United States". Other names for this "Complex" include "The Eastern Establishment" which the great Senator Joe McCarthy took on almost single handedly or quite simply the "They" of "They Live". This is the same "They" with which everyone out here in "the imbecile majority" has an almost Twilight Zone infatuation and wholly unjustified blind faith in.

The original title of this book (which was merely going to be link on my web site www.boxofsunglasses.com) was to be "AIDS and the Doctors of Death". It was taken from an excellent book by "conspiracy theorist" and medical doctor Alan Cantwell who is one of only a few vociferous medical professions insisting the AIDS virus *has* to be man made (it's actually a whole, happy family of oddball viruses; more on that later). Well that's preposterous. How could "They" imagine "They" could away with such a thing? "They" would never try this. This is the United States most if not all bought and sold media stuffed shirt hot air zombie shills both "conservative" and "liberal", would say. Technically "They" are correct, in a physical sense. This is America geographically at least. But when "They" threw (God and) the babies out (literally with the anti-born alive

Barack Obama currently keeping the chair behind the Oval Office desk warm) with the bath water all bets were off. Without God, the real One, what really separates us from say Nazi Germany? Do you think all those genocidal wackos in the radical environmental movement calling man "a cancer" are playing around? The religious environmental movement is the vehicle of justification for what amounts to mass murder. (See Their Lists page on the web site for starters when you're done here)

AIDS is *just one* example of how "They" have been trying to cull in the herd so to speak as "They" seek to create some kind of anti-Garden of Eden here on "Mother Earth". Mass experimentation on us out here in "the imbecile majority" is quite common. UN-fortunately this isn't "conspiracy theory" but documented by "our" very own Federal Government, as you'll see in the Appendix.

(Also please note it is not my intent to recreate the wheel; the reader is invited to research these topics with my sources and my sources' sources provided at the end to his/her satisfaction.)

Continuing, please don't lump me in with those idiot so-called "Christians" who claim that AIDS is some kind of Divine punishment from God, the real One, towards the homosexual community. If you're reading this right now be aware that we're still in the age of grace where *any* sin has already been paid for courtesy the Crucifixion of Jesus Christ, the real One. These people quite simply are all too willing to "cast the first stone" just like the throngs of Jesus' day who would have stoned the prostitute to death without His simple requirement, "let he who is without sin cast the first stone".

And also I would like to separate myself from the "useful idiots" out there like current Communist in Chief Obama's so-called "Christian" pastor Jeremiah Wright and the other American (i.e. God) hating wackos. Just as a stopped clock is correct twice a day this guy has a valid point when he says AIDS was man-made and originated right here in the (Godless) "Late Great USA". But that's where my agreement with this guy ends and here is why he's well one big "useful idiot":

1. His "black liberation theology" is essentially intertwined with the Nation of Islam. The core belief of the Nation of Islam is that there was a superior black race in the distant past we need to bring back that is exactly the same belief as Adolf Hitler's pursuit save the skin color. (And this is one of his smarter moves).

2. This whole AIDS effort (and more) comes under the umbrella of eugenics and population control. Another major subset of this umbrella was and still is abortion. And not only does he support "a woman's right to choose" he supports Obama who believes live babies should be allowed to wither and die. And abortion is rooted in Hitler inspiration Margaret Sanger's self proclaimed "negro project". So yes he's supporting an industry whose goal is to eviscerate the American black (and as you'll see supported by many of the same names behind the AIDS fiasco. So yes this guy is that dumb).

3. When his racially charged sermons became national news Barack Obama threw him under the bus without hesitation. Yet this moron can't see Barack Obama was using him as a political convenience in Chicago as he still throws his support behind "the One" even though "the One" threw him under the bus. Go figure.

4. If you espouse the black version of the purity of the Aryan race how do you support a guy whose mother was white and was raised mostly by his white grandmother in a white middle class setting? This idiot can't even get his racism right.

Let's move on.

I. Background

a. "The Strecker Memorandum"

When I was an undergraduate student studying microbiology as part of my civil and environmental engineering degree a semester long report was assigned as part of the course requirement. I had come across "The Strecker Memorandum" from some friends who said something like "you've gotta see this". I watched and was intrigued. At the time, the late eighties, AIDS was front page news. Some monkey had bitten an African native and whammo a new plague was upon us. But Doctor Robert Strecker had a unique view: this whole thing was no accident. It came out of the microbiology labs of these very United States. Albeit he was very much in the minority I decided to make "AIDS" the subject of my report and check on the unknown Doctor Robert Strecker's claims. (As an aside please note the "AIDS Virus" name is somewhat misleading, AIDS is the result of an attack on the human body by virus known as HIV, Human Immuno Deficiency Virus). Doctor Robert Strecker seemed to be telling the truth but I need to check the sources and the sources' sources (i.e., remember "The Doubting Thomas" concept).

What I found was absolutely shocking and confirmed what Mr. Strecker was saying. Everyone in the scientific world was openly admitting that "AIDS" came from cows and sheep, not African Green Monkeys like "They" were telling us. So one must ask the first simple question, "why"? Why would "they" blatantly lie to the public?

1

Additionally, this wasn't supposed to happen. Virologists and related scientists discuss something called "the species barrier". In a nutshell, viruses are very picky on the living entities and even the cells they attack, i.e., they're "host specific". And now we were being asked to believe that "AIDS" (and four other related viruses) had performed this 'hat trick' just like that.

And Doctor Strecker produced documents from the UN-dead's World a-hem Health Organization and our very own Department of Defense requesting studies and actual "AIDS" like viruses be produced in vitro, in the lab, unnaturally. I dug much of this information up on my own, independently and corroborated what he was claiming. Examples of this documentation are presented at the end of this book in the Appendix.

The first response most people will have to this shocking reality is crazy, never in this country, kook, crackpot, ad nauseam. And after a while I caved and started to listen to my detractors which consisted of just about everyone I had told what it was I found out. My "AIDS Crusade" to try to get the truth out was short lived. This then will be my first goal: document the sordid history of "The Late Great USA" as far as its efforts to assist perhaps the most famous genocidal maniac in history, one Adolf Hitler. When one looks at this reality along with the shenanigans of the American gang banker complex of genocidal maniacs led by Rockefeller family interests with an open mind one would in fact *expect* something similar to an AIDS genocide to occur as the next logical step in their Hitlerean march to world domination by centralized government control and genocide.

And it all ties back to the three warnings I have been repeating incessantly:

1. BEWARE THE ENVIRONMENTAL MOVMENT: it has nothing to do with legitimate environmental problems and is rooted in "Mother Earth" worship.
2. The real "THEorY of LIVEvolution" has nothing to do with the Darwinian Dumbos and their walking, talking fish that nobody can find or DNA producing random explosions but with mankind's spiritual evolution and re-connection with "Mother Earth" minus a few billion "useless eaters" (see Warning Number 1).
3. Watch out for this guy Barack Obama/Barry Soetoro/Barack Hussein Obama II/whatever his real name is.

Finally, *I know personally* that the leading god/scientific snake oil salesman of the modern day eco wackos knows about this whole fiasco as I delivered a mountain of information including a copy of "The Strecker Memorandum" to his Senate Office Headquarters in Nashville, Tennessee. This was back in my naïve days when I still had a picture of an American Government that acted on behalf of its citizenry.

So it was no surprise that aside from a short letter thanking me and promising to look in to what I had placed in his office I never heard from Senator Albert Gore again.

b. The Pristine Bullet

The assassination or more appropriately the execution of John F. Kennedy may be the most studied and controversial murder in world history. It was covered in Section 2b of "The THEorY of LIVEvolution" not to mention copious books on both sides of the issue. One side would be the lone gunman theory mostly perpetuated by The Establishment and its fake left liberals and equally fake neo con windbag conservatives. On the other side are the "conspiracy theorists" including yours truly.

It's without question that JFK, not unlike the great Joe McCarthy a decade earlier, was making enemies in high places in "The Establishment" or what ex-President Eisenhower dubbed "the military-industrial complex". Two of the top reasons for this animosity would be JFK's signature on something called Executive Order 11110 that legalized the United States Treasury to mint silver metal coins that did not have to be borrowed from the "Federal" "Reserve" (It's not federal, there are no reserves). This monetary scam is thoroughly discussed in Section 2b of "The THEorY of LIVEvolution" with many of the same names covered here including Rockefeller and Carnegie lurking behind it in the shadows. Of course this couldn't go on because the proles out here in "the imbecile majority" would start to ask stupid questions like what exactly is "the Fed"? Or try this one: tell me again why we need a shady, private bank issuing fiat currency back to us...at interest?

The other reason JFK became persona non grata with The Establishment is that he started having misgivings about an erupting war in a small southeastern Asian country few had heard or cared about. The stated goal of Vietnam was to stem the tide of Communism but in the end all it did was waste or ruin literally tens of thousands of lives and indebt us to "the Fed" billions of more dollars...with interest. Think about it: the country was lost anyway as the military was hamstrung by disgraceful politicians (and The Establishment mouthpiece Walter Cronkite) yet some 15 years later Communism was (we were told) contained with the collapse of the Berlin Wall.

Oops.

This was covered in Section 2c of "The THEorY of LIVEvolution" as well. Additionally, the nefarious David Rockefeller admits in his own "Memoirs" that he was trading with Communist Central, the Soviet Union, who were turning right around and feeding the North Vietnam

Army who then killed those in the United States military (see the Reviews page on my web site).

Oops.

Put this all aside for a second and think objectively for a second. And forget about all the other information you've heard about JFK's untimely demise. "Lone gunman" and mediocre marksman Lee Harvey Oswald supposedly got off three rounds (a feat the best marksman in the world had trouble repeating) on that fateful day. One missed and hit a nearby curb. One literally blew off the back of JFK's skull. So that leaves one (3 − 2 = 1) round left. This one round is credited with causing multiple wounds in both JFK and Texas Governor Connally who was riding in the front seat of JFK's limo. This one round also would have had to literally twist and turn mid-flight to do this in blatant disregard for Newton's First Law hence the "Magic Bullet" scenario illustrated wonderfully in Oliver Stone's "JFK" movie.

And it gets 'better'. This round was found in nearly perfect condition on a stretcher at Dallas Parkland Hospital where JFK's body was taken after the shooting scene. The problem was that the fragments pulled from JFK and the Texas governor *weighed more than this bullet itself.* So now not only was this bullet "magic" it was "pristine" as well as it appears to be the only round in history to defy the Law of Conservation of Mass.

But "They" formed the Warren Commission (a bunch of Rockefeller Empire shills which will be discussed later) and it was Oswald; had to be. This is the United States and things like that don't happen here.

Nothing to see here; keep moving.

The goal here is not to solve JFK's murder; chances are it will never be solved. The goal is to get you to think independently. If this scenario involved some celebrity or average member of "the imbecile majority" you bet the crime would be solved.

But here nothing was solved. All we have is a bullet that defies basic laws of motion and the Law of Conservation of Mass. This isn't "conspiracy theory", they're basic scientific facts. If you're a Rush Limbaugh "dittohead" or 'opposition' "liberal" and buy in to this crock of ..... and think it can't possibly happen here because well just because then you're probably wasting your time here and in fact my entire website.

For those who are hopefully a little more inquisitive read on to see what "They" have been up to.

b. "The Order"

Another concept to keep in mind is "The Order", the Order of Skull and Bones. It's another bane of "conspiracy theorists" like yours truly that goes even deeper than what will be discussed here. That such an organization exists is beyond question; even the History Channel had a decent expose on it. Member George H. Bush even admits to it in his autobiography albeit in only one sentence. It was covered in Section 2i of "The THEorY of LIVEvolution" and other places throughout the web site. It stresses the Hegelian Dialect whereupon "The State" rules above all regardless of "conservative" or "liberal" pundits and so-called "experts" disagree on. This opens a whole other aspect of "the conspiracy". For now suffice it to say that "The Order" sits above any individual aspect of "The UN-American Complex" including the Rockefeller circles of power and the CIA. In fact, the CIA term "spook" arises from the fact that so many CIA types came out of "The Tomb" at Yale University. "The Tomb" is the ultra-secretive "spooky" home of "The Order" where all kinds of weird activities centered on devil worship and coffins is among the family friendly activities undertaken by the "conservatives" like George H. and W. Bush, late writer and neo icon William Buckley and opposition "liberals" like Massachusetts Senator John Kerry. Hmmm. Maybe this explains why the label changes from "Republican" to "Democrat" or vice versa in the District of Criminals do not really matter. Nothing ever really changes except that Debt Clock in Times Square gets an additional column representing another order of magnitude added to it.

You do realize it doesn't matter at this point...don't you?

Let's return to the task at hand, "The UN-American Genocidal Complex". To prove yours truly isn't just spouting off some nut-job paranoia or "right wing hatred" let's carefully document some background on the sorted past of the *Godless gang banker controlled* "Late Great USA" and then talk about basic virology and the miracle "species jump" of at least five animal viruses that showed up relatively suddenly. Yes, 'AIDS' is actually a family of at least five animal viruses. The studies and experiments to get there really originated in the ghoulish experiments of Nazi Germany that in turn got its start right here in "the Late Great USA". And speaking of the Nazis they're as good a place to start as any.

II. Adolf Hitler: An American Gang Banker Creation

This seemingly outlandish concept is covered extensively In Section 2c of "The THEorY of LIVEvolution" and the **Theosophy** link on the RC Christian page of my web site. The fact that this concept keeps popping up indicate just how very difficult it is to separate the Aryan nightmare from the current "conspiracy" overtaking "The Late Great USA". However, for convenience I will delve into this subject once again, albeit summarily, since it establishes the backdrop for the (seemingly) astonishing claim of the man-made origins of AIDS.

a. Financial

It's well established historical fact that Standard Oil subsidiary and post World War I German industrial giant IG Farben was THE backbone of the Nazi war effort in the second "war to end all wars". That's Rockefeller family owned Standard Oil. This is not an accident nor it is an accident that the Rockefeller name keeps popping up in the upcoming Orwellian slave state economic calamity known as "the Late Great USA" (hopefully you've already played "the Rockefeller Game" prior to getting to this point). IG Farben's industrial capacity reached far and wide and included the production of synthetic oil from coal for the fuel and synthetic rubber for the tires that carried the German Wehrmacht to kill millions including the poor slobs in the United States military. Additionally, Zyklon B which was used to murder untold thousands in Nazi concentration camps was produced by the chemical arm of IG Farben. Not by coincidence one of the original board members of IG Farben was Max Warburg. Max was brother to Rothschild money man Paul who, along with American banksta criminals JP Morgan, Andrew Carnegie, John Rockefeller and their associated minions, was behind the "Federal" "Reserve" scam that's still in existence as you read this (and in fact the source of "your" money). The Warburgs represented even the Rockefeller's bosses, Rothschild money interests from Europe but that's a whole other story. Another American company that essentially made the Nazi war effort a reality included General Motors whose German subsidiary Opel produced German tanks, likely the ones that ambushed near frozen American GIs in the December 1944 surprise attack known as the Battle of the Bulge. Other American companies that 'assisted' the German war effort included Ford, ITT, Dow Chemical and IBM which helped categorize and organize the mass deaths in the concentration camps. This egregious situation is summarized on the back cover of late historian and "conspiracy theorist" Anthony Sutton's "Wall Street and the Rise of Hitler":

Professor Anthony Sutton proves that World War II was not only well planned, it was also extremely profitable- for a select group of insiders. Carefully tracing this closely guarded secret through original documents and eyewitness accounts, Sutton documents the roles played by JP Morgan, TW Lamont, the Rockefeller interests, General Electric Company, Standard Oil, National City Bank, Chase and Manhattan Banks, Kuhn, Loeb and Company, and scores of other business elitists. (1)

In his book Mr. Sutton also thoroughly documents the shenanigans of the American gang bankers at the time. And ho-hum the Rockefeller owned National City (later Chase-Manhattan) Bank and criminal cohort JP Morgan and his minions are all over the American to Nazi loans and investments that grew Hitler's war machine. For example:

In brief, in synthetic gasoline and explosives (two of the very basic elements of modern warfare), the control of German World War II output was in the hands of two German combines created by Wall Street under the Dawes Plan.
In brief, American companies associated with the Morgan-Rockefeller international investment bankers – not it should be noted, the vast bulk of independent American industrialists – were intimately related to the growth of Nazi industry. It is important to note as we develop our story that General

Motors, Ford, General Electric, DuPont and the handful of companies intimately involved with the development of Nazi Germany – except for the Ford Motor Company – controlled by the Wall Street elite – the JP Morgan firm, the Rockefeller Chase Bank and to a lesser extent the Warburg Manhattan bank. This book is not an indictment of all American industry and finance. It is an indictment of the "apex" – those firms controlled through the handful of financial houses, the Federal Reserve Bank system, the Bank for International Settlements, and their continuing international cooperative arrangements and cartels which attempt to control the course of world politics and economics (2)

As an aside notice the current (2009) home of the internationalists, the Bank for International Settlements or BIS, dubbed "the Tower of Basel". It's at the core of the Rockefeller/JP Morgan descendants of the "conspiracy" whose aim is to eviscerate the "Late Great USA" out of existence via the "Federal" "Reserve" System as you read this. But let's not get sidetracked with annoying details.

Just in case you don't want to take "conspiracy theorist" Anthony Sutton's (he is certainly not alone) word here let's get well known historian and Bill Clinton mentor Carroll Quigley in his own words to corroborate this information right out his 1000 page plus history book entitled "Tragedy and Hope".

A brief background is in order before proceeding to Mr. Quigley's book. The first "War to End All Wars" or World War I was occurring. The United States was neutral. That was until "Progressive" shill President Woodrow Wilson, who several years earlier had signed in to law today's "Federal" "Reserve" scam, went back on his campaign pledge (geez talk about a broken record) to keep the US out of what was essentially a European territorial and nationalist war. The impetus for involvement was the sinking of the US cruise ship/floating ammunition dump known as the Lusitania. The result of the so-called "Great" War was gang banker attempt at World Government number 1, the League of Nations which was the predecessor to the UN-dead. What happened in post World War I Germany which then was called the Weimar Republic was an economic situation known as hyperinflation, the academic name applied when the adolescent in charge of the bank in Monopoly hands out too much paper money. Baltic and Broadway don't acquire more 'value' instantaneously because of any legitimate economic demand but their price increases simply because there's more paper money instantly available. What happened in

9

the Weimar Republic was the result of a few basic factors. The Treaty of Versailles limited Germany's exports and demanded it pay 'reparations' to its former adversaries including France. They soon began defaulting on these payments that angered France which in turn took the industrial Ruhr Valley by force further crimping down on the Weimar's ability to generate revenue. Additionally, the German government itself was unwilling to tighten its belt and maintained the fake standard of living by printing money which as I just explained is really no different than some joker handing out "free" money in a game of Monopoly. Or a certain crumbling ex-country coming soon to a neighborhood near you.

By the way if this situation sounds familiar....

Anyway let's get back to Mr. Quigley. Enter stage left JP Morgan and the rest of the criminal banksta cartel. "They" would rescue the Weimar Republic from its economic malaise or so the "experts" would have us believe. Charles Dawes was a JP Morgan operative which would be like Al Capone's lieutenant showing up to help the local business solve its economic problems:

The Dawes Plan, which was largely a J.P. Morgan production was drawn up by an international committee of financial experts presided over by the American Banker Charles G. Dawes. It was concerned only with Germany's ability to pay...

...Specifically, Germany was able to borrow abroad beyond her ability to pay, without the normal slump in the value of the mark which would have stopped such loans under normal circumstances. It is worthy of note that this system was set up by the international bankers and that the subsequent lending of other peoples' money to Germany was very profitable to these bankers.

Using these American loans, Germany's industry was largely re-equipped with the most advanced technical facilities...

...Moreover, the foreign loans which Germany borrowed could never have been made but for the reparations system. Since these loans greatly strengthened Germany by rebuilding its industrial plant, the burden of reparations as a whole on Germany's economic system was very slight (3)

In other words Germany was an economic basket case as a result of the "Great" War partially by its own doing and partially by the Treaty of Versailles. The "solution" was to have the American gang banker criminals led by JP Morgan artificially prop them up post-hyper inflation during which time its industry was re-built. The first plan was called the Dawes

Plan and when this didn't work out another plan was developed called the Young Plan named after its founder, General Electric operative Owen Young (Keep this thought in mind). And in all this economic malaise during the time known as "The Roaring Twenties" in the soon to be "Late Great USA", one Adolf Hitler and the National Socialists or Nazis came to power.

This is the "Cliff Notes" version of post World War I Germany but it serves as an important piece of the puzzle. So as not to get too off track "conspiracy theorist" Anthony Sutton succinctly summarizes what actually manifested as a result of all this American Wall Street banksta chicanery:

This American assistance to German cartels has been described by James Martin as follows: "These loans for reconstruction became a vehicle for arrangements that did more to promote World War II than to establish peace after World War I" (4)

Recall one of the biggest "cartels" was Rockefeller owned Standard Oil subsidiary IG Farben.

Of course asking how this is possible other than some kind of historical 'accident' (nothing to see here, please keep moving) makes you a "conspiracy theorist" or an outright "conspiracy kook".

b. Religious Beliefs

This is easy; sort of. In a nutshell, no pun intended, Adolf Hitler took The "THEorY of LIVEvolution" to its literal conclusion or tried to anyway. Essentially he accelerated, or tried to, what the Darwinian Dumbos claim is (Godless) nature's job. The "science" of evolution is so bad it cannot be considered science but in fact religion: it's so contradictory to established LAWS of science including Newton's Laws and The Laws of Thermodynamics that its ONLY purpose is to eviscerate God, the real One. Additionally, he drew from a wide array of American and English pseudo-scientific religious types most notably Helena Blavatsky, founder of a religious belief called Theosophy, closely related to Gnosticism, the "religion" of the Freemasons represented by the 'G' in their symbol.

Let's start with Ms. Blavatsky. It's no coincidence that the swastika is showed prominently on the front cover of "Madame" Blavatsky's best known work, "The Secret Doctrine". Ms. Blavatsky also happens to be widely regarded as the founder of the modern "New" Age Movement here in the "Late Great USA". Well that's funny; Adolf Hitler and the "New" Agers run in the same religious circles? In a word, yes.

This concept involves a whole new discussion but for now suffice it to say that Adolf Hitler's main goal was to recreate a "Great White Brotherhood" that once existed in a place called Tula. Essentially this was a place one in the same with "Legendary" Atlantis which in turn was pasted by a certain worldwide Flood event or deluge.

If this is starting to sound familiar it should, it's the "story" of Noah and the Flood; a "story" that happens to pervade almost every culture in the world.

So what's the relevance here? In Section 3 of "The THEorY of LIVEvolution" I make the case that the modern "New" Age Movement is nothing but re-packaged Ancient Egyptian and Babylonian paganism. Today (2009) the main subset of the "New" Agers is the radical environmental movement who worship Gaia, the Greek's "Mother Earth" Goddess, one in the same with the Ancient Egyptian goddess Isis.

And when you peek behind the elitist supporters of the eco wackos like Maurice Strong, Al Gore, Ted Turner, Bill Gates, David Rockefeller, George Soros, etc. of today one can quickly see its main goal isn't about saving "Mother Earth" at all. In a word its main goal is genocide.

Does this mean that your run of the mill low level member of the Sierra Club or even the UN-dead is into genocide? No. But they're running interference for those behind them like the Rockefeller Foundation, the Carnegie Foundation, the Tides Foundation, etc. whose predecessors, as we've just seen, actively supported Adolf Hitler and now support them, the modern day Gaia worshippers. So one must ask why would the mega-industrialist Rockefeller, Carnegie, et. al Foundations support those that should be their main opposition?

The only answer this "conspiracy theorist" keeps coming up with is the same: genocide.

The other half of Hitler's religious belief system traces back to the same religion of the Freemasons, the knowledge or "Gnosticism" (i.e., the Freemason "G" displayed so prominently on many of their signs and temples) that man can become God, the real One. This is the REAL goal of the "evolution", mankind "evolving" into Godhood. Again if this sounds familiar it should; it's the same lie the serpent or Satan told Eve in the original Garden of Eden, "ye shall be as gods".

So once again the Christian Bible that so many post-modernist Darwinian Dumbos would cast off as old fashioned and outdated aligns with some of the most prominent figures in modern history, and the "New" Age Movement.

Continuing, another religious pursuit Adolf Hitler was obsessed with was a pursuit of the Holy Grail. This put him in direct competition with a mysterious Russian mystic by the name of Nicolas Roerich. Roerich in turn was working for the Franklin Roosevelt Administration in a real life historical saga that reads just like an Indian Jones novel. Another indicator of Hitler's obsession of the "Holy Grail" was a group that was intertwined with the early Nazi Party, the Teutonic Knights. This group was a direct descendant of the Knights Templar. As discussed in other portions of my web site including the RC Christian page the "History Channel" Knights Templar that were formed to protect "pilgrims" traveling from medieval Europe to the Holy Land were vastly different than the actual Knights Templar who were pursuing their own version of "The Holy Grail". Out of the Knights Templar came the inspiration for the British Round Table Groups. These British Round Table Groups were the ones who started the American's own Council on Foreign Relations or CFR, the bane of "conspiracy theorists" like yours truly. It's no coincidence that the CFR has included those who have always run in the same circles as the Rockefeller-Morgan-Carnegie cabal of criminal bankstas (i.e., the ones behind one Adolf Hitler). So once again the same names keep popping up.

Of course not everyone is privy to becoming God, the real One. Only those who can "evolve" have this capability. Well if you're Adolf Hitler you have to be a white northern European of Nordic or similar stock. If you're Helena Blavatsky well it's pretty much the same group. She herself in "The Secret Doctrine" talked of "savages" in places like sub-Sahara Africa that would never be able to ILLUMINATE themselves with the "sacred spark" or "divine spark" that mankind can become God, the real One. Notice the term ILLUMINATE as in "Illuminati"; this is by no means a coincidence. For example the serpent also told Eve "your eyes shall be opened". And where do we see, no pun intended, the most controversial open eye today? Right, the "Great" Seal on the back of "your" "Federal" "Reserve" note. This is not a coincidence by any stretch and lies at the core of the ILLUMINATI "conspiracy".

In summary, the key to man turning into God, the real One, started in the Garden of Eden and has manifested itself in outright lunatics and genocidal maniacs throughout history. For purposes of this book one of those happened to be Adolf Hitler who intended to fully re-create the Garden of Eden right here on Earth if given the chance. And thanks to the American gang banker cartel of genocidal maniacs he very nearly did.

No matter our genocidal maniac ILLUMINATI criminal masters move on. Having discarded the Bohemian corporal "They" came up with the UN-dead and its globalist American bashers, devil worshippers, eco spiritual weirdoes and WHO death merchants running interference for their ultimate goal: genocide for the re-creation of the Garden of Eden or what the "New" Agers would call the "Age of Aquarius" as they all re-connect with "Gaia".

This is the *religious* background. So where does the 'rubber' of Hitlerean religious beliefs hit the 'road' of physical genocide like the Holocaust? Once again, the "Late Great USA" serves up the answer.

c. Eugenics

The American eugenics movement can be broken down into two basic halves, race hygiene and abortion. Let's start with race hygiene.

i. Race Hygiene: "To That Great Leader, Adolf Hitler"

Hitler's practice of "race hygiene" started right here in the "Late Great USA" plain and simple. Once again this is what happens when man tries to become God, the real One. The Founding Fathers tried to warn us and gave us a system of governance based on the inherent evil of mankind.

But the criminal gang bankers and scientific freaks right here in the 'ol US of A would have none of that (play the Rockefeller Game for starters). As "the conspiracy" essentially controls the mindless garbage that comes out of the idiot box from Desperate Housewives to the fake resistance neo-cons of FOX sNEWS and liberals of C(ircus)NBC allow yours truly to run briefly through some facts to corroborate this disturbing but unfortunately accurate historical situation.

"Race Hygiene" is the same exact term employed by the Nazis as they sought to essentially clean out the human race of the "feeble minded", "misfits" and "morons" in order to create the aforementioned "Great White Brotherhood" of "Legendary" Atlantis. UN-fortunately the same names keep popping up as New York Times writer and "conspiracy theorist" Edwin Black laments:

Indeed, the Rockefeller Foundation helped found the German eugenics program itself. The corporate philanthropy built key eugenic laboratories from the ground up, paid for scientific studies, subsidized travel, financed journals and extended lucrative fellowships to German eugenicists – all to continue research into America's racist notions of biology. The fruits of this research were to be implemented in Europe. (5)

Many of these "eugenic laboratories" consisted of various branches of the Kaiser Wilhelm Institutes including the Institute for Brain Research and the Institute for Anthropology, Hereditary and Race Hygiene. And what served as the foundation of "racist notions of biology"? Why none other than the THEorY of LIVEvolution. So it's no coincidence that in the mid-nineteenth century two of those instrumental in revving up the American "race hygiene" movement were none other than Charles Darwin's son Leonard and Cousin Francis Galton.

In 1904 American banksta types associated with the Carnegie Institution and Harriman Rail Road interests funded a new laboratory at Cold Spring Harbor in Long Island, NY. It's still in existence today. Definitely keep this name in mind. Its first director was a guy by the name of Charles Davenport. Out of this so-called scientific lab emanated journals and other information related to the American eugenics movement. It was (is?) the very nexus of American eugenics. Interestingly within its corridors was something named "the Station for Experimental Evolution". Another subset of Cold Spring Harbor was something called the Eugenics Record Office (ERO) also started by Mr. Davenport. One of the scientific magazines that originated in this laboratory of mass death was Eugenical News. So what did this magazine get involved with? Here once again is "conspiracy theorist" Edwin Black:

German race analyses of American society were always well received. In May 1927, Eugenical News reported the introduction of a German "race biological index" to eugenically rate different ethnic groups for value to mankind. The article repeated German warnings of "the danger of an eruption of colored races over Europe, through the French colonies (in Africa) and colonial troops". In the article, German researchers urged "further studies in America, both of Indians and American negroes, as compared to those still living in Africa" (6)

Mr. Black also notes that ..."Germany had achieved preeminence in both legitimate genetic research and spurious racial biology". Much of this brainpower came about courtesy Cold Spring Harbor, USA. This is all very interesting as the case is made for the man made origin of HIV/AIDS from places like Cold Spring Harbor.

So what kind of unsavory characters did Charles Davenport and his Cold Spring Harbor and American eugenic cohorts eventually hook up with? One would be the "Angel of Death" himself, Adolf Hitler's very own Josef Mengele:

Charles Davenport, who headed up Carnegie's Cold Spring Harbor Headquarters, was equally inspired by Verschuer. On December 15, 1937, he asked Verschuer to prepare a special summary of his institute's work for Eugenical News, "to keep our readers informed." Davenport also asked

Vershuer to join three other prominent Nazi eugenicists on Eugenical New's advisory committee. Falk Ruttke, Eugen Fischer and Ernst Rudin were already members. With a letter of gratitude, Verschuer agreed to become the fourth. Verschuer was now an essential link between America eugenics and Nazi Germany.

Otmar Freiherr von Verschuer had an assistant. His name was Josef Mengele. (7)

Other entities that started popping up in this whole American-Nazi German eugenics love fest included "The International Population Congress" and the "International Federation of Eugenics Organizations". "Conspiracy theorist" and author Stephen Kuhl wrote another excellent book on this subject entitled "The Nazi Connection: Eugenics, American Racism and German National Socialism". In it he quotes an American eugenicist by the name of Clarence Campbell at the 1935 version of the International Population Congress:

"To that great leader, Adolf Hitler".

By 1935 Auschwitz was already in its third year and Hitler's infamous "Mein Kampf" had been written around 10 years before that.

In the late nineteenth century a poor Aborigine was put on display at the Bronx Zoo as proof to "the imbecile majority" that Darwinian evolution was true. These people really believe this stuff; "They" aren't screwing around.

Mr. Black again illustrates this very poignantly:

No matter how dismal the plight of the Jews in Germany, no matter how horrifying the headlines, no matter how close Europe came to all out war, no matter how often German troops poured across yet another border, American eugenicists stood fast by their eugenic hero, Adolf Hitler. (8)

Hey this only gets better. Let's take a quick look at another American Adolf Hitler hero, the "Progressive" Margaret Sanger. You wouldn't even have to get to "Race Hygiene" if you just aborted the poor bastards right out of existence to begin with...

ii. Birth Control: "The Negro Project"

As stated, for the most part "Race Hygiene" can be considered one-half of the Hitlerean eugenics/population control movement. The late Margaret Sanger best represents the other half, birth control. Ms. Sanger was the founder of The American Birth Control League, precursor to today's Planned Parenthood. She was considered a "Progressive" and was involved with all kinds of left wing radicals in her day including Emma Goldman. This woman was pure evil.

But don't take my word for it. With the backdrop of the recently documented American-Nazi love fest let's get Ms. Sanger in her own words, right from her autobiography:

...Recently it (eugenics) had cropped up again in the form of selective breeding, and biologists and geneticists such as Clarence C. Little, President of the University of Maine, and C.B. Davenport, Director of the Cold Spring Harbor Station for Experimental Evolution, had popularized their findings under this heading.

I accepted one branch of this philosophy, but eugenics without birth control seemed to me a house built upon sands. It could not stand against the furious winds of economic pressure which had buffeted into partial or total helplessness a tremendous proportion of the human race. The eugenists wanted to shift the birth control emphasis from less children for the poor to more children for the rich. We went back of that and sought first to stop the multiplication of the unfit. This appeared the most important and greatest step towards race betterment. (9)

Take note of who she's meeting with, Andrew Carnegie's own Charles Davenport, the first chairman of Cold Spring Harbor. Of course we wouldn't need Mr. Davenport and his disciples like Nazi big wigs Ernst Rudin and Josef Mengele if the "feeble minded" and "imbeciles" didn't exist to begin with. Besides outright genocide of the so-called "unfit" Adolf Hitler was in to all kinds of selective breeding of his beloved Aryan German race. But just to be sure of this woman's rancid beliefs align perfectly with one Adolf Hitler let's get her beliefs in her own words:

There is but one practical and feasible program in handling the great problem of the feeble minded. That is, as the best authorities are agreed, to prevent the births of those who would transmit imbecility to their descendants.

Feeble mindedness, as investigations and statistics from every country indicate, is invariably associated with an abnormally high rate of fertility. Modern conditions of civilization, as we are continually being reminded, furnish the most favorable breeding ground for the mental defective, the moron, the imbecile. (10)

Hmm. This sounds like someone whose award I would be proud to receive like say the wife of the "first black president" one Hillary Clinton, the self admitted "Progressive". Or even better Obama's so-called science czar who advocates sterilizing welfare recipients and "green abortions". Of course Ms. Sanger's philosophy, just like her protégé Adolf Hitler, is directly opposed to Jesus Christ, the real One. And she doesn't pull any punches here:

I have touched upon these various aspects of the complex problem of the feeble- minded, and the menace of the moron to human society, not merely for the purpose of reiterating that it is one of the greatest and most difficult social problems of modern times, demanding an immediate, stern and definite policy, but because it illustrates the actual harvest of reliance upon traditional morality, upon the biblical injunction to increase and multiply, a policy still taught by politician, priest and militarist. (11)

Every one is aware that Adolf Hitler's most publicized target was Jews. But they only comprised half of his "Race Hygiene" handiwork. The other half consisted of well "... the mental defective, the moron, the imbecile,..."; in his eyes at least. He, just like Freemason "New" Ager Theosophist Helena Blavatsky, was no fan of blacks either. Margaret Sanger (and Hillary Clinton and John Holdren for that matter) could easily have sat at a table with these two (Hitler and Blavatsky). Again here she is in her own words advocating for something called "The Negro Project":

It seems to me from my experience where I have been in North Carolina, Georgia, Tennessee and Texas, that while colored Negroes have great respect for white doctors they can get closer to their own members and more or less lay their cards   on the table which means their ignorance, superstitions and doubts...The ministers work is also important and also he should be trained, perhaps by the Federation as to our ideals and the goal we hope to reach. We do not want word   to get out that want to exterminate the Negro population and the minister is the man who can straighten out that idea if it ever occurs to any of their more rebellious members. (12)

Read that last sentence again. Yet "Progressive" Hillary Clinton proudly accepts the Margaret Sanger award. And (half-white) "Progressive" Barack Obama goes beyond the duplicitous Hillary as he voted *against* something called The Born Alive Infant Abortion Protection Act. And of course both come under the evil and treasonous Rockefeller umbrella. That name keeps coming up again and again: I repeat it's behind anything to do with de-populating to the planet not to mention the outright destruction of this once great country from Adolf Hitler to Barak Obama (for starters see the **1984** link on this web page).

Among Ms. Sanger's top backers was the Rockefeller Foundation. That name *again*?

III Post World War 2

a. Vatican Ratlines

The Catholic Church's sorted past includes a very UN-God like resume. This 'resume' includes an almost 2,000 year suppression of many of the civilized world's poor, the massacre and mass murder for God (in their eyes at least) known as the Crusades and the outright murder of so-called heretics who dared question them known as the Inquisition. Now we can add to this resume of disgraceful behavior support and outright assistance to escaping Nazi war criminals (not to mention support *prior* to World War II but that's another story). The so-called ratlines ferreted away some of Hitler's best and brightest and most evil. Author Dave Hunt discusses this egregious situation in his book "A Woman Rides the Beast". Here are some excerpts in regards to one, but certainly not only, prominent member of the Catholic Church that supported Nazism, Bishop Alois Hudal:

> *One of the early key figures directing the escape of Nazi war criminals (and especially Catholic clergy) was Bishop Alois Hudal, rector of seminary for German priests in Rome and a close associate of both Monsignor Giovanni Montini (later Pope Paul VI) and Alcide de Gasperi (later Italian Premier).*
> *Hudal saw no conflict between his beloved Roman Catholicism and his equally beloved Nazism.*
> *…Equally favored by the Nazis, Hudal held a Golden Nazi Party membership badge.*

Among the war criminals that Hudal helped escape were major figures such as Franz Stangl, commandant of the infamous extermination camp at Treblinka; he presided over the efficient murder of about 900,000 inmates, mostly Jews.

Stangl was finally located and recaptured in Brazil in 1967 by Simon Wiesenthal's Nazi hunters, who learned of the Ratlines. This underground network of Catholic offices, seminaries, convents and residences provided not only shelter on the escape route but false identities and passage to South America and other safe havens. The most famous mass murderer of them all, Adolf Eichmann, atheistic head of the SS Department for Jewish Affairs and in charge directly under Hitler of the entire Holocaust, was among the tens of thousands who were carefully smuggled by Catholic officials with Vatican blessing down the Ratlines. (13)

The Catholic Church didn't act alone. It had help, not surprisingly, from the American Intelligence complex including the newly formed Central Intelligence Agency.

b. American Intelligence

The intent of this section is to tie American Intelligence to the UN-American Genocidal complex. Like so many other topics I discuss whole books have been written on this subject alone not to mention copious information on "the information superhighway" of the internet. What I've done here is present the information in a 'birds eye' view, a palatable read that summarizes the task at hand. Now let's proceed.

The thing, for lack of a better word, known as American Intelligence post World War II is a spider web of complexity which has one overall goal in mind: control of all humanity. This control comes via mind control (i.e., the "They Live" scenario) and literal control of populations (i.e., the UN-American genocidal complex). Let's start with a brief history, and then discuss each of these separately before tying it all together.

i. Background

The Central Intelligence Agency or CIA was officially formed in 1947 as the successor to the World War II era Office of Strategic Services (OSS). The OSS counted among its members one David Rockefeller. So it should be no surprise that the newly formed CIA immediately tied very strongly in to another Rockefeller dominated organization, the Council on Foreign Relations (CFR). The CFR, which is nothing to worry about according to neo con windbags like Rush Limbaugh, is thoroughly documented in Section 2 of "The THEorY of LIVEvolution". Very briefly, the CFR was derived starting in the late nineteenth century from its British counterpart, the so-called Round Table Groups that emanated out of globalist central, Oxford University. It formed officially in 1921. It is dominated by "globalists" and "globalism" as any simple perusal of their website will indicate. Its magazine Foreign Affairs has been a mouthpiece of 'globalism' for years. Getting back, author and "conspiracy theorist" Jim Marrs summarizes the CIA-CFR relationship:

Demonstrating how every US government administration since the Council's inception has been packed with CFR members, conservative journalist and CFR researcher James Perloff noted, "The historical record speaks even more loudly....Through 1988, 14 secretaries of state, 14 treasury secretaries, 11 defense secretaries and scores of other federal department heads have been CFR members."

Nearly every CIA director since Allen Dulles has been a CFR member...

Many researchers have alleged that the CIA, in fact, serves as a security force, not only for corporate America (my addition read: Rockefeller oil interests, JP Morgan owned GE, etc.) but for friends, relatives, and fraternity brothers of the CFR. This may be a two way street. According to a former executive assistant to the deputy director of the CIA Victor Machetti along with former State Department analyst John D. Marks, "The influential but powerful Council, composed of several hundred of the country's top political, military, business and academic leaders, has long been the CIA's principal 'constituency' in the American public. When the agency has needed prominent citizens to front for its proprietary companies or for other special assistance, it has often turned to Council members." (14)

ii. Mind Control

The centerpiece of the CIA's mind control endeavors was something called MK-ULTRA. Its studies of human mind control were quite diverse. First, they included studying the effects of drugs on humans including barbiturates and LSD. Second, it included non-drug mental manipulation with hypnosis and telepathy. In fact the term 'brain-washing' was derived from these efforts. Continuing, sometimes these experiments were combined in their ghoulish attempts to control other human beings for nefarious purposes. The 'publicly' stated reason was to keep pace with those pesky Soviet Communists but this in itself is brain-washing: the Soviet Communist Bolshevik "revolution" was an American gang banker creation with the usual cast of characters including the Rockefeller family right in the middle. So as not to go off on this tangent this concept was covered extensively in Section 2 of "The THEorY of LIVEvolution". Besides, the current Rockefeller banksta criminal leader Davie, writes in his own "Memoirs" that he's "proud" to be an "internationalist" and that he was trading with the Soviet Union while the poor slobs in the Marines were taking it on the chin from...the Soviet Communist supplied North Vietnamese.

But then again we're drawn right back in to this whole seemingly contradictory mess as Rockefeller operative and CIA director Allen Dulles is the one who ordered MK-ULTRA in to existence in April of 1953. This guy was Rockefeller insider all the way so do you think he knew a thing or two about the *real* Soviet Communist "enemy"? And interestingly enough he was to stand before the great Joe McCarthy and his committee but somehow was able to weasel out of it courtesy The Establishment and its CFR Oval Office Seat Warmer "President", Dwight Eisenhower.

The sister operation to MK-ULTRA was something called Operation Paperclip. This effort ferreted out Nazi scientists before they got to the dog and pony show Nuremberg Trials in a parallel and sometimes joint effort with the aforementioned Vatican Ratlines. These guys were a hot commodity for not just us but our enemies turned friends back to enemy again, Mother Russia. These Nazis, who had gotten their queue from the American eugenics movement as explained earlier, had several years and several million live subjects that had been under study; there's no way all this scientific data could be thrown to waste. Most of the rest of us know these human study centers as Concentration Camps. The name "paperclip" was derived from the fact that the new whitewashed histories of these otherwise genocidal maniacs were often paper-clipped to their personnel files in order to avoid any 'problems'.

Operation Paperclip spin-offs included names like "Apple-pie", "Eclipse" and "Project 63". This last one placed ex-German Nazi scientists in top positions at Lockheed, Martin Marietta and North American Aviation. It is particularly ironic in that a few short years earlier these companies were producing American planes whose intention was to knock these bastards back to the stone-age. Now they were not just our friends but top researchers.

Makes you wonder, doesn't it? Maybe "They" (LIVE) were (are?) utilizing Mind(ON'T QUESTION AUTHORITY) Con(FORM)trol o(BEY)n us poor slobs o(BEY)ut here in the A(CCEPT)merican "(NO) i(NDEPENDENT)mbecile majorit(THOUGHT)y".

Hold that thought, no pun intended.

iii. Population Control: Henry Kissinger and Friends

There's obviously a lot more to the whole UN-American Genocidal Complex than just one man, albeit a very powerful one both in and out of the public eye for decades. But tracking this inner circle Rockefeller operative helps to cull a lot of information together in a relatively short summary. In the Appendix are located images of actual documents where the UN-dead's World a-ahem Health Organization and the United States Department of Defense requested an HIV like plague. On the surface this effort was to find a theoretical cause of cancer in humans, viruses. These types of studies began in the mid 1960s at which time the WHO got itself involved in all kind of genetic and cancer causing virus research fun; the kind of "fun" you'll see later in this chapter. It formed alliances with other members of the UN-American Genocidal Complex including the National Institute of Health, Center for Disease Control (CDC) and the Army's biological warfare testing center at Fort Detrick, Maryland. This sorry state of affairs is documented in multiple books included in the sources cited at the end. In "Emerging Viruses" Dr. Leonard Horowitz describes one of the outcomes of the genetic freak show undertaken by the UN-holy alliance of members of the UN-American Geoncidal Complex:

In essence, they developed AIDS like viruses by the early 1970s. Their stated purpose was to alter a host's genetic immunity allegedly to control cancer. Experiments were designed to produce an assortment of lymphocytic leukemias, sarcomas, and opportunistic infections in chickens, mice, rats, sheep, cats, monkeys, and humans. (15)

And who was in the center of this overall effort in the "late 1960s"? President Richard Nixon's National Security a-hem "Advisor" and Rockefeller operative Henry Kissinger. And what was one of the central themes of this Rockefeller operative and the guy keeping the chair behind the Oval Office desk warm? Why none other than genocide umm "Population Matters" as Doctor Leonard Horowitz quotes 'ol Tricky Dick:

The president, in his Message to the Congress on Population Matters of July 1969, and then again in 1971, appealed for more urgent action. Secretary of State William P. Rogers quoted the president who said:

"...few subjects will so deeply affect the lives of this and future generations as the challenge of population growth. It is important also that we recognize the need to meet this challenge with an extreme sense of urgency. The momentum already built into the world's population growth means that delay in acting now will greatly increase the burden of all the problems which must be borne later. (16)

There's more here but you get the point: 'ol Tricky Dick and his Standard Oil operative Henry Kissinger could have worked for the "liberal" eco wacko global warming/global cooling/climate change crowd over at the UN-dead (not a coincidence by the way). A little bit later on Dr. Horowitz quotes "Tricky Dick" and his efforts in conjunction with the World Health a-hem Organization to eliminate disease in Central Africa via widespread vaccination programs. Not coincidentally many of these vaccination programs just so happen to align geographically with the soon to be viral explosion that seemingly came from nowhere known as HIV/AIDS.

By the way did I mention that the Godless, devil worshipping eco-wacko freaks known as the UN-dead was founded by Rockefeller family money? Speaking of the UN-dead one of the books I discussed in my book "The THEorY of LIVEvolution" that's in the middle of the whole population control/eco wacko scam emanating from the UN-dead is entitled "Beyond Interdependence". The Foreword and Introduction were written by David Rockefeller and his genocidal associate and global elitist ('eco rules are for the little people that we decide can live') the "Canadian Al Gore", Maurice Strong. Keep an eye on that word "interdependent" as Dr. Horowitz quotes Hank Kissinger who somehow survived the whole Tricky Dick debacle as speaks to the House Committee on Foreign Affairs on June 4, 1974:

Americans have a vital stake in the realization of this prospect. In a world made interdependent – by nuclear weapons, instant communications, and global economy –Americans can preserve their security, their values and their prosperity only by nurturing the shoots of stability and cooperation. Our policies are shaped by that purposes...(17)

As an aside let's look at UNFPA, the United Nations Fund for Population Activities, and another piece in the cog known as the UN-American Genocidal Complex. At around the time of the whole Tricky

Dick/Kissinger/let's not forget Vietnam debacle in the late sixties this fund was involved in1200 "population projects" in 100 countries according to Dr. Horowitz. Who was among those funding the Fund? No one in particular, just the same recycled names exposed by the great Joe McCarthy in the previous decade and the same names behind today's genocidal maniac radical environmental movement, the Ford and Rockefeller Foundations.

:( )YAWN.

Ol Henry who surprise, surprise taught at Harvard excuse me HAAARverd and served as a paid consultant of Rockefeller owned Chase Bank, was right in there with another Rockefeller, Nelson. Former Oval Office seat warmer and now I guess one would have to say "conspiracy theorist" President Dwight Eisenhower warned of the "military-industrial complex" which would of course include the pseudo military organization CIA and its sister organizations like the National Security Administration (NSA) and left over Operation Paper Clip types. So from Eisenhower we went to JFK and as we'll see shortly he got on the wrong side of "The Establishment". From JFK it was on to Lyndon B. Johnson who got steamrolled by "The Establishment" as anyone who has seen him holding his head in utter remorse near the end of his tenure as "President" will attest. But then it was Nelson Rockefeller versus a re-tread from the political scrap heap due to his loss to the now executed JFK. That re-tread known as "Tricky Dick" somehow took the election from Nelson. No problem, Henry was on the scene to keep the globalist genocidal ball of death rolling right along as he became "Tricky Dick's" National Security Advisor.

Another quick 'fun fact', simultaneous with Hank Kissinger's time with Tricky Dick a graduate of "The Order" was running the CIA, future Oval Office seat warmer and "advisee" George H. Bush who used the term "New World Order" in public probably for the first time. Surely he knew a thing or two about "The Order" since his father Prescott worked hand in fist with the American Criminal Banksta Cartel/eugenics big wigs including Harriman rail road interests that helped fund the Nazis.

Dr. Horowitz summarizes old Henry Kissinger:

In summary, Kissinger was at the center of a good old boy intelligence network even before the Ford and Rockefeller Foundations funded his International Seminar, I realized (18)

Gerald Ford waltzed in as Oval Office Desk seat warmer after "Tricky Dick" and his former VP Spirew Agnew were deep sixed for crimes that are peripheral to this discussion. Due to this historically unique situation, Mr. Ford was the only one who ever achieved "President" without a vote. With all the action associated with Watergate, Vietnam and the general shadiness of the UN-American Genocidal/Military Industrial Complex coming to light an investigation was in order. What better way to sedate "the imbecile majority" back to its zombie like existence (STAYASLEEP OBEY CONFORM DON'T QUESTION AUTHORITY) than stick them with another whitewash committee of Rockefeller shills. This situation is summarized by yet more "conspiracy theorists" who see through the UN-American Genocidal Complex documented in a book entitled "AIDS: The Crime Beyond Belief":

With Vice President Ford established as President of the United States, it was time to elect a 'safe' Vice President. Who better for the job than Nelson Rockefeller, former Assistant Secretary of HEW and later special consultant on CIA activities under President Eisenhower? When Ford was asked why his Rockefeller Commission had so many right wing, shadowy military/intelligence members on it, he replied in a private off the cuff answer that it was to make sure no embarrassing questions were asked. When asked what subjects he meant by 'embarrassing' he replied Assassinations for example.

Rockefeller did the job, and by hanging out some totally unexpected dirty laundry he caught his critics off guard with the Rockefeller Report on CIA Excesses' and so took the edge off demands for even more rigorous investigation of CIA mis-deeds. (19)

Poor Nelson lost out in the race for "President". But not to worry, an obscure peanut farmer would end up on the covers of the Rockefeller controlled disgraceful mainstream snews that would lead to the disaster known as the Jimmy Carter Administration under the guise of Rockefeller puppy dog and Trilateral Commission (who? See Section 2 of "The THEorY of LIVEvolution) co-founder Zbigniew Brzezinksi.

Just like the awful series of movies "Night of the Living Dead" which is up to 8 or 9 this guy Kissinger, and for that matter Columbia University professor and Barak Obama teacher/ "advisor" Zbigniew Brzezinski, keeps getting recycled. You can still catch the dinosaur Henry Kissinger on "conservative" FOX sNEWS from time to time. This is no surprise as another Rockefeller operative, Rupert Murdoch of the Bilderberg Group, runs the fake "conservative" right of "The Order" with squeaky clean efficiency. Whoa the what? The Bilderberg Group is another part of the UN-American Genocidal Complex. It was founded by the Rockefeller consortium together with a Prince Bernhard from the Netherlands. Now WHO is this guy? Well this Prince was in the Nazi SS and an employee of IG Farben, which, as discussed previously, was the Rockefeller Standard Oil subsidiary that built the Nazi war machine.

Boring.

What's relevant to today, 2009, is that the Prince was an early day eco wacko that today resides behind the global warming/global cooling/climate change fiasco:

This is exactly what he labored towards in the next 40 to 50 years. Under the guise of environmentalism, the prince founded the 1001 club in 1970 with the aim of raising funds for the World Wildlife Fund (of which Bernhard was the first chairman, and top-eugenicist Julian Huxley was the founding father).

Now, with Copenhagen in full swing, we are seeing exactly what the elitist environmental movements have worked towards: the creation of a global Leviathan.

Not by openly routing nation-states would the global designs of the New World Order be accomplished (which would after all only incite uprisings and rebellion), but rather by sneaking in through the United Nations, World Bank and other tentacles of global governance. (20)

By the way aren't we talking American Intelligence (no joke here)? How the hell, pun intended, did we get here?

iv. The Warren Commision and "Dr. Mary's Monkey"

This whitewash collection of Rockefeller associated criminal banksta, political and CIA types warrant a brief discussion in light of the aforementioned Pristine Bullet. Again, the intent here is not to re-create the whole Kennedy "conspiracy theory" circus and other circumstances related to his untimely demise. But let's look briefly at some of the characters that were part of this sham that was UN-American Genocidal/Military-Industrial Complex all the way. Here's the list of its members:

Earl Warren, Chief Justice of the Supreme Court
Richard Russell, US Senator (D-GA)
John Sherman Cooper, US Senator (R-KY)
Hale Boggs US Representative (D-LA)
Gerald Ford, US Representative (R-MI)
Allen Dulles, former director CIA
John J. McCloy, former president World Bank

These so-called 'powerful' men were subservient to the Rockefeller Complex (that in turn is subservient to "The Order" of Skull and Bones; more on that later).

Let's start with Earl Warren. He was chosen by ex-World War II General and President Dwight Eisenhower for the Supreme Court. Generally thought of as a so-called moderate he turned out to be a liberal "Progressive", the same movement that worked hand in fist with the American and Nazi eugenicists in the early part of the twentieth century. He had ties to another Rockefeller, Nelson Aldrich (related to the same Senator Aldrich who produced the legislation for the shadowy "Fed" in 1913) through New York Governor Thomas Dewey. Dewey was a so-called "liberal" Republican (gee where have we heard this term before?) who ran in the same circles as Nelson Rockefeller and was supportive of anti-American institutions including Roosevelt's so-called New Deal that came about as a result of the "Great" Depression that in turn came about because of the policies of "the Fed". This was even admitted to by current 2009 Fed Chairman Ben Bernake as I thoroughly document in Section 2b of "The THEorY of LIVEvolution".

But let's not get sidetracked with annoying details.

Dewey ran as a presidential candidate against Harry Truman and was unsuccessful. Besides supporting the Franklin Roosevelt "New" (more aptly raw) Deal, that many economists now claim worsened the Depression, Dewey was supportive of another Rockefeller founded institution, the UN-dead. Governor Dewey was succeeded by Nelson Aldrich Rockefeller in New York.

Let's look at Gerald Ford. His claim to fame was that he was the only president that ever became president without being elected. This came about since both Richard Nixon and his Vice President Spirew Agnew were cast out by The Establishment. Nixon's political career had been considered DOA when he lost the presidency to none other than JFK but somehow came back to life when his offices moved close by the Rockefeller consortium right here in MYSTERY, BABYLON umm New York City. This comeback from the dead was not unlike the sudden rise of a peanut farmer from Georgia who came from nowhere thanks to The Establishment and an Arkansas "Progressive" who didn't inhale and a Chicago vagabond "community organizer" who miraculously rose through the ranks yet still can't figure out which hospital he was born in yet had another meteoric rise to Oval Office Occupier under the guise of his ex-teacher, "advisor" and Rockefeller boot-licker Zbigniew Brzezinski. By the way, didn't this discussion start out talking about ex-Supreme Court Justice Earl Warren?

Do you see how hard it is to separate "the conspiracy"?

We briefly discussed Gerald Ford's brief acquisition of Oval Office Occupant. Suffice it to say he was a Bilderberg Group attendee (WHO?) in 1964 and 1966. The Bilderberg Group is another Rockefeller founded operation that meets in relative secret every year since its inception in 1954. It includes the most powerful international players in finance, education, entertainment, news (this "conspiracy theorist" makes a compelling case that these last two are the same), etc. That such a thing exists is admitted to rather openly by...wait a second...TA DA...Davie Rockefeller in his "Memoirs" (see Reviews page on my web site). It was covered extensively in Section 2k of "The THEorY of LIVEvolution".

Let's move on.org, pun intended, to speak for George Soros, another criminal banksta genocidal maniac in the Rockefeller circle of power who lives as the ultimate capitalist pig yet is somehow a "liberal" and supported by "useful idiot" minions like moveon.org.

Allen Dulles was an interesting character. This guy, not unlike his Warren Commission cronies, was Rockefeller all the way. As previously mentioned he was head of the CIA. Prior to this he served in the CIA's predecessor, the OSS. Additionally, he and his brother John served as lawyers for the Rockefeller Standard Oil Company (which has since morphed in to all kinds of companies most notably Exxon-Mobil). Also, it was on Dulles property that the foundation of the American (and Nazi inspiring) eugenics movement was built, "Camp Cancer" umm Cold Spring Harbor (which we'll get to in the next section). Cold Spring Harbor was originally funded by American criminal bankstas Andrew Carnegie, Averill Harriman and TA DA...John D. Rockefeller. The Dulles brothers weren't shy about voicing their support for Rockefeller's support of finding the "perfect human nature". Of course Rockefeller money also poured in to support another Adolf Hitler inspiration and "negro project" founder, the genocidal maniac Margaret Sanger. And of course the Dulles property's Cold Spring Harbor which was heavily involved in the Rockefeller's sick Darwinian "survival of the fittest" medical research is right in the middle of the whole AIDS/HIV fiasco as we'll see shortly. While we've just mentioned Charles Darwin it turns out that the Rockefeller Institute of Medical Research (now Rockefeller University in New York City) had a Rockefeller founded German counterpart known as the Kaiser Wilhelm Institute that would serve as that country's foundation for another genocidal maniac who had the nerve to take Darwin's (and Maggie Sanger's for that matter) racist views and put them in to practice. That guy's name? Adolf Hitler...whose scientists came here courtesy Operation Paperclip as just mentioned.

Isn't this fun?

While we're still on it we should mention that another University of Chicago 'humanist' Godless Rockefeller operative, no not Barack Obama, by the name of John Dewey came about around this time along with the precursor to the way left wing National Education Association, the General Education Board. These sell-out institutions were targets of "tail gunner" Joe McCarthy. Another was Allen Dulles. He was supposed to appear before the great Joe McCarthy who was looking in to all of these shenanigans but was able to get out of it courtesy CFR member and President Dwight Eisenhower.

So, as I've documented endlessly, the greatest politician since perhaps Abraham Lincoln has at least one fan out here in "the imbecile majority".

John J. McCloy was another Rockefeller operative who ran family financed operations (well not really since this "financing" comes courtesy of the "Fed" which really produces funny money or fiat currency but let's not get sidetracked with such trivial matters) including Chase-Manhattan

Bank (which was a combination of Rockefeller's Chase with fellow "Federal" "Reserve" criminal Paul Warburg's Manhattan Bank).

I can go on with this but the point has been made: These are the guys that invented the only bullet in human history to contravene Newton's First Law AND the Law of Conservation of Mass. Enough said.

Another factor that should be entered in to this equation is the shadiness surrounding the seedy characters tied to Lee Harvey Oswald and monkey viruses in New Orleans. This crowd included religious loner and CIA associated David Ferrie, businessman Clay Shaw and ex-FBI agent Guy Banister. Banister had direct connections to the patsy Lee Harvey Oswald, the CIA and the whole anti-Castro movement. This whole scary scenario is spelled out in a new book by author and "conspiracy theorist" Edward T. Haslam. Just the front cover of the book indicates the magnitude of what's discussed

Dr. Mary's Monkey

How the Unresolved murder of a doctor, a secret laboratory in New Orleans and cancer-causing monkey viruses are linked to Lee Harvey Oswald, the JFK assassination and emerging global epidemics. (21)

Whew. I need a break and we haven't even gotten past the front cover.

The overall point of the book is to establish that "They" screwed up with the polio vaccine that was administered in the late 1950s under the auspices of Doctor Jonas Salk and current VP, Richard Nixon. Basically, the vaccines were cultured in monkey kidney cells and this is where a new monkey virus escaped, undetected, in to the vaccines and from there directly to the blood of millions of American children. Mr. Haslam takes more of the accidental approach as to a whole generation of kids being exposed to cancer causing monkey virus known as SV-40 (Another good reason to run away from the Big Pharmaceutical death jabs known as vaccines. The whole current Swindle Flu vaccine swindle is covered in the Swin(dl)e Flu link on my web site).

Accidents do happen as may have been the case here. But this bunch, the UN-American Genocidal Complex, is not investigating genetic engineering and adapting animal retroviruses to humans for its health, no pun intended. Although the author doesn't mention Henry Kissinger by name Rockefeller dynamic duo Allen Dulles' along with his brother John name appears multiple times throughout. So it's no surprise the following passage indicates another example of the shadiness of those involved with the UN-American Genocidal Complex:

The ill-fated polio vaccine which NIH released during Nixon's Vice Presidency (1953-61) killed one of Ochsner's grandsons and temporarily crippled his granddaughter. The publicity about the bad vaccine outraged the public and caused a political debacle, toppling the Secretary of Health, Education and Welfare and routing the leadership of NIH. Entering the office of President in 1969, Nixon promptly declared "War on Cancer", quadrupled the budget of the National Cancer Institute, converted the Army's biological warfare center to a cancer research laboratory, and financed the NIH's "Viral Cancer Program" (22)

'Ol "Tricky Dick" would have been taking 'advice' from his Rockefeller operative National Security Advisor one Henry Kissinger. Interestingly enough Mr. Kasalm talks about "the sudden and massive outbreak of AIDS among American homosexual males..." (that will be discussed in Section V, AIDS and the Doctors of Death). For now let's get his take on the seedy origins of "the gay plague" that popped up out of nowhere in six specific cities here and simultaneously popped out of nowhere as a heterosexual disease in central Africa:

In order to be considered a possible creator of HIV-1, one would have had to possess both the capability of mutating a monkey virus and the opportunity to do so within the established timeframe.

Let's analyze capability first. If you were going to mutate a monkey virus, the first thing you would need is access to monkey viruses! Where would you get them? Drug stores do not sell monkey viruses. A zoo may have monkeys, but if you asked the zookeeper which one had a given retrovirus, he would not be much help. The obvious answer to "Who would have had access to monkey viruses?". The people who were doing medical research on monkey viruses!

So let's make the question explicit: Who was researching monkey viruses during the late 1950s and early 1960s?

In fact, there was a small group of medical schools, private laboratories, and government research facilities here in the US, and a smaller number in Europe and the USSR. The majority were among those facilities which specialized in either genetics or cancer research. (23)

Whether he realizes it or not Mr. Haslam just summarized the UN-American Genocidal Complex save the UN-dead's World a-hem Health Organization. And notice the USSR bit. All of the medical doctors/ "conspiracy theorists" that I reference in this article discuss a shady Soviet microbiologist named Wolf Szumness. This guy managed to 'defect' from the Soviet Union with his whole family (which never happened in real life except for this guy) and landed at gang banker central, Columbia University. From there he ended up behind the Hepatitis B vaccination program that just so happens to match the onset of "the gay plague" here in "The Late Great USA" in 1979. Of course cooperating with the 'enemy' Soviets is no problem for David Rockefeller and his operatives like Henry Kissinger as I have Davie in his own words aiding and abetting the Soviets (see Reviews page on my web site) who were in turn aiding and abetting the North Vietnamese while we were supposed to be fighting a so-called war against Communism that JFK, whose murder was whitewashed by another group of Rockefeller operatives, was actively trying to stop. Whew.

Isn't this fun?

So again I must ask: with all this Rockefeller cronyism going on is it any surprise that "They" invented the only bullet in history that contravened both the laws of motion and conservation of mass when investigating the murder of the only President since Abe Lincoln to seriously challenge the gang bankers?

Speaking of that Lincoln assassination....ah different subject; kind of.

v. Back to the Nazis

In the last quote from the previous part was the term "...genetics or cancer research". And what was among the programs of study the Operation Paperclip Nazis (remember with their American eugenics foundation) were studying? Vaccines and genetics supported by some names you should be familiar with by now. Doctor Leonard Horowitz summarizes the situation:

The NAZI Party, led by Joseph Goebbels, and Adolf Hitler, favored vaccinations for producing the "master race." NAZI eugenicists, financially and ideologically advanced thanks to global drug industrialists operating through the Rockefeller and Carnegie families' foundations, considered vaccinations a leading (most profitable) technology for genetic modification, blood intoxication, health degeneration, and population reduction. This technology was considered essential to maintain economic control in the wake of burgeoning labor unions and immigrant populations that posed threats of revolutionary uprisings. For Hilter, Goebbels, NAZI doctor Mengele, and the Rockefeller-led eugenicists, the "Big Lie" included the need for "public health" measures, including vaccinations, that could be used to kill and pharmaceutically-enslave people. (24)

So what was the outcome of the Nazi "underground railroad" known as the Ratlines courtesy the Vatican and their American Intelligence Nazi supporting allies? Don't worry it only gets 'better'.

c. Eugenics (THEY LIV)Evolves Into Genetics

Son of a Holocaust survivor, author and New York Slimes umm Times correspondent Edwin Black has written extensively on the American eugenics-Nazi connections (he is the only positive I can see out of that disgraceful rag of our criminal banksta elite but that's another story). This introduction to one of his chapters can apply to today's Health 'Scare' umm Care debate or the December 2009 Copenhagen Summit that "our" illustrious leader Barack Obama has decided to attend to 'solve' the scientific scam known as global warming/global cooling/climate change. The latter is covered in Part IV, Religious Environmentalism. But let's not get ahead of ourselves. Here's "conspiracy theorist" Edwin Black summarizing the progressive, genocidal elites of the early twentieth century, the same ones at the time knowingly giving ideas and inspiration to one Adolf Hitler:

A phalanx of shock troops sallied forth from obscure state agencies and special committees – everyone from the elite of the academic world to sympathetic legislators who sought to shroud their racist beliefs under the protective canopy of science. In tandem, they would hunt, identify, label and take control of those deemed unfit to populate the earth (25)

Those in charge of these "shock troops" included Cold Spring Harbor founder one Charles Davenport. Recall that Cold Spring Harbor came in to being with funding by JP Morgan fellow gang banker Andrew Carnegie money and land donated by the Rockefeller minion Dulles brothers.

Of course real science and "Inconvenient Truths", pun intended, like the Constitution and widespread public resistance out here in the "imbecile majority" (to quote another "New" Age Hitler inspiring elite by the name of Helena Blavatsky), didn't matter to the genocidal minded elites of the Davenport American eugenics era. Now all you would have to do today, December 2009, is to replace the names of the Nazi loving scientists "Davenport, Laughlin..." with names like eco charlatan Al Gore, Obama's "science czar" John Holdren, Gaia hypothesis author /Club of Rome operative James Lovelock and recently ousted climate change charlatan Phil Jones of England's East Anglia University and you have a very accurate description of the radical environmental movement: its goal of population control being carried out by sell-out politicians who have little time for "the imbecile majority" all being covered underneath a thin veneer of so-called science emanating from the so-called "experts" at the UN-dead and Harvard excuse me HAAARverd.

Trains were the main mode of transporting Jews and other Nazi undesirables to the concentration camps. Here's some more from Mr. Black who has tracked, no pun intended, the eugenics to genetics death train from Auschwitz to New York City's own UN-dead courtesy its conductors, the Rockefeller Complex and friends:

After Hitler, eugenics did not disappear. It renamed itself. What had thrived loudly as eugenics for decades quietly took postwar refuge under the labels human genetics and genetics counseling. (26)

Soon you'll hear about "Camp Cancer". For now realize that early studies of eugenics invariably spilled over in to outright attempts at genetic manipulations of humans themselves. UN-fortunately as you've already seen and will see again the manipulation of human genes along with the creation of veritable witches' brews of plant, virus, bacteria, etc. genes would become commonplace in the decades following the early twentieth century establishment of the foundation of such evil, Cold Spring Harbor.

All it takes is some gang banker seed money and voila a whole class of so-called "experts" emerges to solve the world's problems (i.e. too many inferior people) in the name of science; Godless science that is. During the early twentieth century genetics and eugenics were taught as part of the curriculum in many schools. Of course the foundation of this "conspiracy" in education was camouflaged by the originators of the American eugenics movement way back in the mid 1800s, Francis Galton and Leonard Darwin. Yes, he was the son of the same Charles Darwin of "evolution" fame and ever the hero of today's Darwinian Dumbos like Oxford "scientist" Richard Dawkins and "comedian"/bought and sold political hack Bill Maher. (For a thorough debunking and the REAL purpose of "evolution" take the "No God Allowed Evolution Challenge" on the home page of my web site, boxofsunglasses.com). In an event that substantiates this whole mess the magazine "Eugenical News" was changed to "Current Record of Human Genetics and Race Hygiene" in 1929.

Of course the parallel situation of elites culling in the herd today would be the global warming/global cooling/climate change debacle. This is just another re-packaged scam of Rockefeller-UN-dead elites telling the world it needs to deep six several billion "useless eaters". What's interesting is that in 1938 something called the Institute for Human Genetics opened in the city Copenhagen where today's (December 2009) eco wacko elites are flying in on private jets and driving in with stretch limos to tell the rest of us we have to go to save the planet from global warming/global cooling/climate change. The Institute for Human Genetics has been absorbed in to the University of Copenhagen and today it stands as one of many institutions studying human genetics. The Institute and many of its early scientists were funded by surprise, surprise Rockefeller Foundation and related monies. Today many similar institutions based on this early model dot the European landscape not to mention the descendants of the eugenics minded Cold Spring Harbor right here in "The Late Great USA". (And please note that I'm not incriminating every geneticist in all of these institutions but unfortunately the good work they have done in fighting disease masks the outright genetic manipulation freak-show that will be discussed later on.)

So Copenhagen must be the EU's answer to our very own eco wacko Progressive elite city, let them (that we allow to live) eat cake San Francisco, California. Here are some more tid bids from Mr. Black's excellent book with the same names popping up once again but now "after" the genocidal Nazis were "defeated":

> *While human genetics was becoming established in America, eugenics did not die out. It became quiet and careful. The American Eugenics Society inherited the residium of the movement.*
>
> *... The AES assumed primacy in organized eugenics in the late thirties. It established a relationship with the Carnegie Institution just as the ERO was being dismantled.*
>
> *In 1947 the remnant board of directors unanimously agreed, "The time was not right for aggressive eugenic propaganda". Instead, the AES continued quietly soliciting financial grants from such organizations as the Dodge Foundation, the Rockefeller funded Population Council, and the Draper fund. The purpose: proliferate genetics as a legitimate study of human heredity* (27)

And what was coming online during this time? Right, Obama's Doctor of Death Ezekiel Emanuel's very own Hastings Institute that in its own words right off "Google" "...is an independent, nonpartisan, and nonprofit bioethics research **institute** founded in 1969". Frederick Osborn was American eugenics all the way, the nephew of a former member of the Second International Eugenics Congress in 1936 (the same crowd that was idolizing Adolf Hitler like some kind of rock star) and himself president of the American Eugenics Society in 1946. And of course he was involved in getting "Federal" "Reserve" notes from the same foundations first created and then exempted themselves from the scam "Federal" "Reserve" system back in 1913; the same foundations that were targeted by the great Joe McCarthy and go by names like Carnegie and Rockefeller.

> *Indeed, by 1967, Osborn's society had become a behind-the-scenes advisor for other major foundations seeking to grant monies to genetic research. Even the National Institutes of Health sought their advice in parceling out major multiyear grants for what was called "demographic-genetics". (28)*

And where are these death merchants studying today, 2009? Right Rockefeller University where I'm sure they're into things like "demographic genetics" and "the complete lives system" like their friends in the rest of the Rockefeller-Kissinger-Obama-Emanuel eugenics/genetics/genocidal freak show. Again, take notice of the term "Population Council". And once again what came out of the Rockefeller founded "Population Council"? Why none other than the Hastings Institute, home to Obama's own "Doctor of Death", Ezekiel Emanuel. So we have not just the global warming/global cooling/climate change Copenhagen eco wacko genocidal maniacs tied in with this guy Soetoro/Obama we have the descendants of the Rockefeller-Nazi complex hiding under the name of Health Scare umm Care Reform as it makes "The Case for Killing Granny" to quote the front cover of gang banker mouthpiece Newsweek, September 21, 2009 (the image had to be removed from the Appendix for copyright reasons but look it up yourselves if you don't take my word for it).

What is another beneficiary of Health Scare umm Care Reform? Why none other than the American purveyor of black genocide, Maggie Sanger's American Birth Control League known as Planned Parenthood. Of course black genocide isn't going to win you many votes especially if you're the wife of the "first black president" (and Bilderberg Group attendee) Bill Clinton, Hillary. Ms. Clinton (also a Rockefeller founded Bilderberg Group attendee) relies on the black vote AND collects the Margaret Sanger Award as she has done on at least one occasion. It gets even worse if you're the first actual black president (who remember is half-white) and voted **against** something called the Born Alive Infant Abortion Protection Act. Hence happy sounding words like "family planning", "the right to choose" and "reproductive health" are thrown about by "our" political a-hem "leaders". But remember where it all started in 1904 and continues today, 2009:

Cold Spring Harbor stands today as the spiritual epicenter of human genetic progress. (29)

Isn't this fun?

And now it gets even 'better'; grab your gear boys and girls let's hike over to "Camp Cancer" a ghoulish, fun place not dissimilar to Camp Crystal Lake of "Friday the 13 th" save "Jason"…

I think.

d. Camp Cancer

Much of the "cancer research" post World War II was done under the auspices of the Nazi war criminals freed from the aforementioned Vatican Ratlines and Operation Paperclip. World War 2 General and future "President" Dwight Eisenhower warned "the Late Great USA" about the "military-industrial complex", roughly the same group being targeted by the great Senator Joe McCarthy. He should have warned us about a future UN-American Genocidal Complex as well. This complex only *begins* with the UN-dead's population control eco wacko freaks that support genocide to help out Gaia. "Conspiracy theorist" Doctor Alan Cantwell sums up the situation of what I am now calling the UN-American Genocidal Complex:

> *There are close economic and political ties between the Army Department of Biologic Warfare, the CIA, the CDC, the NCI, the NIH the World Health Organization and private industry groups such as Litton Industries...The combined military and political power of all these federal and private agencies staggers the imagination.* (30)

Mr. Cantwell describes some activities of the UN-American genocidal complex:

> *During the 1960s, the Army's biological warfare program was largely geared to DNA and "gene-splicing" research. In the late 1960s, President Nixon renounced germ warfare except for "defensive medical research". This "defensive research" continues to the present time, and primarily centers around vaccine development and the genetic engineering of infectious agents capable of infecting large masses of people.* (31)

Throughout his informative book Mr. Cantwell constantly references Andrew Carnegie's and Charles Davenport's Cold Spring Harbor as part nexus of the UN-American Genocidal Complex. For example he discusses a Cold Spring Harbor Conference in Asilomar, California in 1973 entitled "Biohazards in Biological Research" and included "... the most powerful government institutions, the top ranking medical universities and the most influential drug companies in the nation". Here he describes what these 'experts' were involved with:

The cancer researchers coaxed all kind of viruses into laboratory cell cultures. In addition, various viruses were injected or fed into animals for the sole purpose of producing cancer, immunodeficiency, opportunistic infections and a host of other fatal diseases. (32)

The combinations that these scientists got themselves, and now the rest of us, involved with is certainly not for the squeamish and will be discussed in detail later on.

William Campbell Douglass is another Medical Doctor who has misgivings about the magic HIV/AIDS virus, a sort of "flying pig flu" virus (the name assigned to the current Swin(dl)e flu in the link on my web site) that popped in out of nowhere in the late seventies. What I found to be most disturbing, if that's possible, in his book "AIDS: The End of Civilization" was his discussions on the nexus of the whole virus gene mixing and matching 'fun' the cancer virologists and related scientists were having while under the auspices of the UN-American Genocidal Complex. That nexus was Charles Davenport's Cold Spring Harbor Lab; the same entity wrapped up in the middle of the Adolf Hitler inspiring American eugenics movement.

An entity "...referred to by those in the know as camp cancer".

And what came out of "camp cancer" back in the early twentieth century? The Eugenics Record Office, center of the original American Eugenics movement that in turn drives the Health Scare Reform of our current Communist in Chief.

Don't worry folks we'll revisit "Camp Cancer" and friends soon.

Isn't this fun?

e. Barack Obama

Whoa. How did we get here so fast? Well for starters I remind the reader, once again, that this guy voted *against* something called the Born Alive Infant Abortion Protection Act while he was a 'budding star' in the Illinois State Senate. This means essentially that "our" Communist in Chief thinks a live human baby should be allowed to wither and die. Maybe if one decides that they really wanted an abortion the day after their child was born can return to the hospital for some "assisted suicide" now that the Supreme Court has granted "the right to choose". Do I really need to say what kind of "slippery slope" we now reside on? So right off the bat he has already passed with flying colors the Margret Sanger half of the American eugenics movement.

Let's get to the fun stuff, the "race hygiene" half. Do you think that when Obama and his minions talk about "bioethicists" deciding who can be "participating citizens" based on "the complete lives system" that rates human worthiness based on age to save our "limited resources" that they're playing games? (Of course our resources are so limited because Obama's Rockefelleresque gang banker criminal masters have set it up that way but let's not get sidetracked with annoying details.)

"Conspiracy theorist" Anton Cheitkin wrote an excellent piece for Executive Intelligence Review entitled "The Nazi Euthanasia Program: Forerunner of Obama's Death Council". Hmmm. We've already covered a lot of territory that makes this case. Let's further the case. Those Nazi war criminals that weren't fortunate enough to hitch a ride on the Vatican Ratlines ended up in the dog and pony show known as the Nuremberg War Crimes Trials. Mr. Cheitkin cites an interesting passage right from the Nuremberg Trials:

The U.S. National Military Tribunal identified as a prime motive of the euthanasia program, "to eliminate 'useless eaters' from the scene, in order to conserve food, hospital facilities, doctors and nurses for the more important use of the German armed forces". (33)

This the exact same scenario painted by our Communist in Chief and his band of genocidal maniacs umm merry makers on why we need "Health Care Reform" in this country. Obama proposes that "bioethicists" employ garbage like the "Complete Lives System" that bases an individual's worth on their age to see who can get treated so they can become "participating citizens". Of course this is all necessary because we're dealing with limited resources here in "The Late Great USA" because Obama's gang banker criminal masters like David Rockefeller and his minions have literally robbed us blind with the "Federal" "Reserve" scam. And if anyone doubts this is the true intention of anti-born alive Obama's genocidal maniac minions led by the ex-chairman of something called the Department of Bioethics at the US Institute of Health one "Doctor" Ezekiel Emanuel we have Paul Ehrlich, intellectual associate of current "science czar" John Holdren in his own words:

One might think that American scientists, especially biologists, would be using their influence to get the government moving…The establishment in American biology consists primarily of death controllers: those interested in intervening in population processes only by lowering death rates. (34)

Well…I don't know…did he really mean that? This is America and things like that don't happen here. Enter once again stage left Paul Ehrlich a modern Maggie Sanger, inventor of the black (now everyone else) genocide known as abortion:

So the first task is population control at home. How do we go about it? Many of my colleagues feel that some sort of compulsory birth regulation would be necessary to achieve such control. One plan often mentioned involves the addition of temporary sterilants to water supplies or staple food. Doses of the antidote would be carefully rationed by the government to produce the desired population size. (35)

So we would have those that aren't "death controllers" telling the Federal Government to sterilize the public water supply. In his joke book to be taken seriously entitled "The Population Bomb" Mr. Ehrlich also proposes mandatory abortions, family limits and other niceties of Red China all to be enforced by an Orwellian UN-dead sounding "Department of Population and Environment". By the way, I delve into Mr. Ehrlich's book much more deeply on "Their Lists" page of my web site where the true genocidal intentions of the radical environmental movement are laid bare. And of course "Doctor" Ezekiel Emanuel is a member of something called the "Federal Coordinating Council for Comparative Effectiveness Research" which, would have to include those that would

NOT be "death controllers" (i.e. "death controllers" = what most of us refer to as "doctor").

Interestingly enough "conspiracy theorist" Anton Chaitkin discusses many of the same names yours truly discussed back in Section I in regards to the Hitler inspiring and Nazi "race hygiene" supporting American eugenics movement. He then summarizes the post-World War II American-Nazi eugenics effort:

> *After the war, with corpses still smoking in Europe, the eugenics/euthanasia movement laid low for a time, inventing new names for itself such as "social biology" and "the right to die".* (36)

So now Obama is on the verge of implementing the initial stages of Adolf Hitler's "race hygiene" program?

Yes.

Let's make this quick and simple as we trace the American-Adolf Hitler love fest known as eugenics right through to the genocidal maniacs in both the Rockefeller founded UN-dead and the Rockefeller backed Obama administration:

American Eugenics Society 1922 (remember the AES?)>

Merges with Rockefeller family's Population Council 1953 >

Hastings Center source of the euthanasia term "bioethics" founded by "eugenics zealot" Daniel Callahan in 1968 with Population Council money >

Geneticist and "evolutionary biologist" Theodore Dobzhansky was also a chairman of the American Eugenics Society and founder of Hastings Center >

"Doctor" Ezekiel Emanuel and then wife Linda both served as "Hastings Center fellows">

Obama's White House Budget Director Peter Orszag's deputy ensures the Hastings Center that "comparative effectiveness" would be at the center of health care reform. Hastings Center regular Henry J. Aaron, another associate of Orszag opines regularly in support of "comparative effectiveness">

"Doctor" Ezekiel Emanuel's ex-wife and "longtime bioethics collaborator" taught " the death education initiative" for the American Medical Association with sponsorship by billionaire moveon.org "useful idiot" founder George Soros' very own "Project on Death in America">

George Soros, David Rockefeller and his Bilderberg genocidal elites like Warren Buffett, Bill Gates and Ted Turner support anti-born alive Barak Obama>

Umm...this "story" is still being written....

And of course Newsweek, another example of the disgraceful corporate lap dog snews, had on its front cover of September 21, 2009 "The Case for Killing Granny" (see the Appendix).

Right on schedule.

Animal rights wacko Peter Singer who, like Obama's "regulatory czar" Cass Sunstein, believes that animals have more rights than human infants, is also a member of the Hastings Center and founder of the "International Association of Bioethics". Mr. Singer is currently a "professor of bioethics" at Princeton University. Just recently he penned an article for the gang banker shills at the New York Slimes umm Times entitled "Why We Must Ration Health Care" (July 15, 2009). Of course he runs the gamut of reasons, including excessive costs and limited resources but does the animal rights wacko point his pen at his criminal banksta elite masters like David Rockefeller and Hank Kissinger as the cause of these very same "limited resources"?

In a word, no. But I would bet all the soon to be worthless "Federal" "Reserve" Notes in the world that he would hop right on board with his genocidal wacko Nazi like Hastings Center associate "Doctor" Ezekiel Emanuel:

Emanuel and some other movement spokesmen have stated that physician-assisted suicide is not necessary, that life-saving care can simply be denied to the elderly and costs will be saved. This will be painless, supposedly, if the patient is unconscious and is starved to death – starvation being one of the first methods used by the Nazi T-4 killers before gassing was adapted. (37)

49

Mr. Chaitkin is implying that all this is the *precursor* to a revitalized Nazi like "race hygiene" nightmare. While true *on the surface* I will submit that this effort actually *continued unabated* after World War II and now "They" don't even care to hide it anymore. The man made HIV/AIDS virus is perhaps only one example of this. Killing babies born alive would certainly qualify as another.

Isn't this fun?

IV. Religious Environmentalism:
The New Eugenics

This material is presented in multiple places throughout my web site and in Sections 2 and 3 of "The THEorY of LIVEvolution" so what's presented here is a mere summary of the subjects at hand. However, for convenience and to 'keep the flow' they are presented here in abbreviated form.

The concept to keep in mind is that the "science" of the radical environmental movement, while not as bad as "The THEorY of LIVEvolution", certainly gives the Darwinian Dumbos a run for the money. And not by coincidence many believe in both. Ummm...

Anyway, there are two basic purposes of the "science" of global warming/global cooling/climate change. One is to give the eco wacko elites like Al Gore, Ted Turner, David Rockefeller, Mikhail Gorbachev (yes that Mikhail Gorbachev), "Canadian Al Gore" (and worse) Maurice Strong, etc. the cover they need to establish the "emergency" and "security issue" of global warming/global cooling/climate change. The "science" also justifies the remedy, "climate justice" enforced by the same group of UN-Dead death merchants who brought us the AIDS virus.

Without further adieu let's get right to it.

a. Junk Science: The Inconvenient Scientific Method

This brief overview is presented here for convenience; it's discussed much more thoroughly in Section 2e of "The THEorY of LIVEvolution" entitled "The Fake Science of the Radical Environmental Movement and the Eco Wackos". The goal is to establish some key points. First, I don't deny that there are legitimate environmental problems like water pollution, solid and hazardous waste disposal and localized air pollution events like Los Angeles and other cities experience due to a phenomenon known as temperature inversion. In fact these are the types of subjects I studied in school under my civil engineering curriculum. This segues into my next point. The eco wackos led by the high priest/charlatan Al Gorebels don't practice sound science. Their science, much of which comes out of the UN-dead, is only a façade for "the imbecile majority". This facade grants legitimacy for their predictions of dire environmental calamity. Let's look at a couple of specifics to make the point. And we'll use "An Inconvenient Truth", the now infamous movie of the high priest/mega-hypocrite of the modern day eco wacko movement, the one, the only Al "private jet/mansion", Gorebels. (Yes the same Al Gore yours truly contacted almost 20 years ago when this whole AIDS fiasco was front-page news). Mr. Gore claims that CO_2 concentrations are directly correlated with temperature increases. While true Mr. Gore, Conveniently, pun intended, fails to mention that *CO_2 concentrations lag, let me repeat, lag temperature increases.* The reason being that the sun (which the "expert" modelers over at the UN-dead's Inter-galactic Panel of Cosmic Clowns or IPCC Conveniently leave out of their models) causes natural temperature swings, up and down. And when temperatures increase the amount of CO_2 the oceans can hold in aqueous solution decreases and is therefore released not unlike the release of CO_2 when you open a bottle of soda (although for different reasons). So this 'deep sixes' Al Gore's and the rest of the Rockefeller funded eco wacko UN-dead global goofballs by itself. And there's more, much more. But for brevity's sake let's take a look at one more example of junk science of "An Inconvenient Truth". Mr. Gore claims that ocean levels will rise over 20 feet thereby inundating low lying areas and coastal cities. This is a literal order of magnitude (i.e., 10 times) higher than even that collective group of goofballs known as the IPCC or Inter-galactic Panel of Cosmic Clowns. In other words, Al Gore is pulling stuff out of his a**.

So what's the real purpose here? Just look at this comedy act: thirty years ago the eco wackos, including one John Holdren our Communist in Chief's "science czar", were screaming that the earth was going to cool and bring us another ice age due to the ever toxic CO_2, the by-product of human respiration. If you wanted to look at global warming/climate change/global cooling with the scientific method you'd first gather information and data. An example of the gathered information would be:

1. CO2 has much less of an effect on climate than water vapor
2. Water vapor is much more prevalent in the atmosphere
3. Mankind's contribution to CO2 is fractions of a percent of the total when compared to the oceans, volcanoes, plant life, etc.
4. There is no valid data correlation between CO2 concentrations prior to temperature increases. However, CO2 increases after temperature increases due to CO2 release from the oceans – when the earth's temperature increases naturally.

Based on this a scientist without a political axe go grind (i.e., mankind and especially mankind in the United States sucks) would objectively have to say "climate change" is absolutely not an issue.

Basically, these clowns *go in* with the assumption that mankind is evil, unnatural and unwelcome on "Mother Earth. In a nutshell, no pun intended, *this is the exact opposite of the Scientific Method*. This explains why these clowns change from cooling to warming to just "climate change" without missing a beat. (For a detailed analysis if it can be called that of Al Gore's elementary school level "science" book "An Inconvenient Truth" see The Inconvenient Scientific Method link on the new age page of my web site boxofsunglasses.com)

So what then is the real purpose? The answer segues perfectly into the next topic...

b. Operation Genocide: The Club of Rome and Friends

This is another topic covered extensively on the rest of this website as well as Section 3 of "The THEorY of LIVEvolution". In a nutshell, no pun intended, the eco wackos literally regard "Mother Earth" as a spirit and/ or a goddess to be protected even if it costs literally billions of lives. And of course we have gang banker interests funding these eco wackos as these modern day "useful idiots" run interference for the coming Orwellian electronic control grid slave state gulag nightmare. And of course the same names pop up especially those associated with the Nazi supporting Rockefeller family. Don't take my word for it. "Google" some of these wackos like our Communist in Chief's ex-"green jobs czar", the self admitted anarchist and Communist Van Jones' group Center for American Progress and greenforall.org. If you click through you'll see support coming from some familiar names (and targets of the great Joe McCarthy) including the Rockefeller Brothers Fund, Rothschild money front man George Soros' Tides Foundation, the Carnegie Endowment, etc. etc. Or try another one, 350.org based on the "science" of the UN-dead's IPCC that states CO_2 must be held to 350 parts per million or we're all going to fry or freeze to death depending if "global cooling" or "global warming" is the flavor of the week. You can find this one right on the website of the Rockefeller Brothers Fund. So one has to ask why? Why would the greatest business greedy capitalists of the world be interested in funding these eco wackos when they should be mortal enemies? The only answer this "conspiracy theorist" can come up with is control: numbers (genocide umm Family Planning) and political (one world criminal banksta slave state umm globalism). And if you read the piece on Adolf Hitler this should not come as a shock and in fact should be expected. On the new age and Their Lists pages of my website I cite multiple instances of these genocidal eco wacko maniacs and their mega rich criminal overlords in their own genocidal words.

But for convenience let's discuss one strange marriage between our gang banker criminal elite and the eco wackos, the Club of Rome. This group of environmental elitists was formed in the 1960s and since then has given us all kinds of dire predictions about mankind and how he is destroying the earth. One of these dire predictions is mass starvation. This beyond ironic since real starvation is being caused by diverting farmland to grow corn based ethanol (a scam in and of itself) by their bequest to solve the scam of global warming/global cooling/climate change fiasco, another scam which they actively promote!

Ummm yeah; it's as stupid as it sounds; so stupid one cannot logically ascribe it to an accident.

One of the eco wacko brainiacs tied in with the Club is a "scientist" by the name of James Lovelock who came up with a brainstorm known as the Gaia Hypothesis; we'll get back to him in a minute. As I demonstrate with literal pictures on the new age page of my web site, The Club runs in the same circles as David Rockefeller's playground of outright weirdoes, eco freaks, globalists, devil worshippers and tin pot dictator thugs over at the UN-dead. But just to be sure here's the Club in its own words on "the real enemy" (umm look in the mirror):

The Vacuum ● 75

The common enemy of humanity is Man

In searching for a common enemy against whom we can unite, we came up with the idea that pollution, the threat of global warming, water shortages, famine and the like, would fit the bill. In their totality and their interactions these phenomena do constitute a common threat which must be confronted by everyone together. But in designating these dangers as the enemy, we fall into the trap, which we have already warned readers about, namely mistaking symptoms for causes. All these dangers are caused by human intervention in natural processes, and it is only through changed attitudes and behaviour that they can be overcome. The real enemy then is humanity itself.

That is literally page 75 from "The First Global Revolution: A Report by the Council of The Club of Rome". Now that's one group of "New" Agers that sounds like boatloads of fun.

Another group of eco wackos is something called the Council on Environmental Quality. In the mid-seventies this Council combined with the US State Department under the guise of David Rockefeller's and Zbigniew Brzezinski's choice for puppet string controlled occupier of the Oval Office or US President for short, one James Carter. This combination produced something called "The Global 2000 Report to the President" in 1976. The study came about as a result of the mindset put forth by the Club of Rome's shenanigans like those just mentioned. All of the eco wackos who were and still are subservient to the UN-American Genocidal Complex were acting in unison with this mindset of man as "the enemy".

This two tiered approach with the Rockefeller related elites in the UN-American Genocidal Complex on top and the "useful idiots" like Van Jones' Center for American Progress running interference can be considered 'Operation Genocide'. Taking orders from 'Operation Genocide' in the 60s and 70s was current (2009) so called science czar John Holdren and his band of merrymakers. One member of this 'band' was a Holdren associate and "Population Biologist" named Paul Ehrlich. As discussed previously, this brainiac calls what we in "the imbecile majority" know as doctors as "death controllers".

Let's stop and take a look at 'Operation Genocide' put out by the Club of Rome and UN-dead friends to solve the non-existent "Population Bomb". ("The Population Bomb" happens to be another eco wacko book written by the aforementioned Paul Ehrlich, friend of current "science czar" John Holdren. It is reviewed on Their Lists page of my web site). Recall from before the authors of "The First Global Revolution" literally believe mankind is "the enemy".

Now here's the solution to "The Population Bomb" mentality those intellectual associates of "science" czar John Holdren (who himself is caught in the middle of the recent November 2009 climate change/global warming/global cooling email scam). This one comes out of a book put out by The Club of Rome entitled "Mankind at the Turning Point":

In summary, the only feasible solution to the world food situation requires:

1. A global approach to the problem
2. Investment aid rather than commodity aid, except for food.
3. A balanced economic development for all regions.
4. An effective population policy.
5. Worldwide diversification of industry, leading to a truly global economic system.
6. Only a proper combination of these measures can lead to a solution. Omission of any one measure will surely lead to disaster. But the strains on the global food production capacity would be lessened if the eating habits in the affluent part of the world would change, becoming less wasteful. (38)

This is basically the plan/insanity of the eco wackos discussed above. An example of the plan part is "effective population policy" a fancy name for genocide. An example of the insanity is they worry about a world food problem that's exacerbated by another sham known as corn for ethanol to solve yet another sham called global warming/global cooling/ climate change. By the way as covered in Section 2e of "The THEorY of LIVEvolution" the whole "climate change" sham was preceded by the UN-dead lead ozone hole sham that itself served as its own mini-genocide.

Does anyone else see a pattern here?

Again, it all traces back to the same point: genocide. Running parallel to this is top down political economic control of "balanced economic development", a code name for worldwide Communism umm globalism. By the way, this is the mindset of our current Communist in Chief; this the mindset of his crowd that includes the genocidal maniac John Holdren along with Rockefeller operative and "advisor" Zbigniew Brzezinski (for a review of Obama's Columbia University Professor and "advisor" see my review on the Reviews page of my web site).

Let's return to James Carter's "Global 2000 Report". It's the usual 700 page plus sleeper of graphs, "science", dire predictions, mankind sucks, etc., etc. Here are some choice excerpts from the Appendix:

In July 1969, President Nixon sent to Congress a historic first population message, recommending the establishment by legislation of a blue-ribbon commission to examine the growth of the nation's population and the impact it will have on the American future. John D. Rockefeller III, who had started the Population Council, had been urging since the early days of the Eisenhower Administration that such a commission be established. ..

In early 1969, Rockefeller's pressure for a presidential commission was abetted by presidential counselor Moynihan...

One of the most serious challenges to human destiny in the last third of this century will be the growth of population. Whether man's response to that challenge will be cause for pride or for despair in the year 2000 will depend very much on what we do today.

When Congress passed a bill in March 1970 creating the Commission on Population Growth and the American Future, President Nixon named John D. Rockefeller III chairman...

The Commission's conclusion was that no substantial benefits would result from continued growth of the nation's population:

The population problem, and the growth ethic with which it is intimately connected, reflect deeper external conditions and more fundamental political, economic and philosophical values. Consequently, to improve the quality of our existence while slowing growth, will require nothing less than a basic recasting of American values. (39)

The first several paragraphs indicate that familiar Rockefeller name at the core of the UN-American Genocidal Complex. I don't have to explain the implications of the last paragraph, do I? In summary, these eco wackos run in the same circles as the elitist Club of Rome which emanates from the Rockefeller created UN-dead (see also the new age page on my web site).

Today (late 2009) the whole global warming/cooling/climate change scam is exposed as the fraud that it is with the current email scam where human hating political hacks described as "climate scientists" were blatantly 'cooking the books' to meet the Club's genocidal goals. With this backdrop does anyone, outside of a few "conspiracy kooks" like yours truly, see 'Operation Genocide' for what it really is? Is it even skipping a beat in its push for "climate change legislation"? Outside of the fake resistance prescribed by "The Order" on David Rockefeller operative Rupert Murdoch's FOX sNEWS is there any inclination to re-think "climate change legislation" whether through Congress or the current EPA headed by former Socialist International member non-scientist Carol Browner?

Are you starting to get the picture here?

c. The Anti-10 Commandments and the Wedding From Hell

Let's pick up the ball with the Club of Rome and let's emphasize why the radical environmental movement is really the *religious* environmental movement (just in case you didn't catch the front cover of "The THEorY of LIVEvolution"). James Lovelock is a so-called scientist who I found just by running through links on the Club of Rome's web site several months back (around September 2009). He formulated a brainstorm that serves as one of the rallying cries of these Mother Earth worshipping wackos, the Gaia Hypothesis. The basic theme is the earth is a living, breathing organism. To save "Mother Earth", the earth's population should be limited to around one billion people (down from its current 6-7 billion). His solution to global warming/global cooling/climate change is to spray sulfur in to the atmosphere to block the sun since "global warming" is the latest flavor of the week according to these pseudo scientific genocidal maniacs. Speaking of "Gaia" she is literally the Greek "Mother Earth" and ties back to the Ancient Egyptian goddess Isis that in turn is related to a certain golden calf worshipped by His chosen people after He helped them escape from…Ancient Egypt. Recall that event really annoyed God, the real One, to His Chosen People and caused Moses to break the 10 Commandments, if you believe that sort of thing.

And while we're on the subject of the 10 Commandments in Section 3 of "The THEorY of LIVEvolution" I discovered a new friend of humanity, Robert Christian. Robert invested a lot of time and money building the Georgia Guidestones, a series of granite blocks dubbed "The American Stonehenge" located in Elberton, Georgia. And inscribed on these so-called Guidestones is what I have dubbed "The Anti-10 Commandments". They are listed here for convenience:

1. Maintain humanity under 500,000,000 in perpetual balance with nature.
2. Guide reproduction wisely – improving fitness and diversity.
3. Unite humanity with a living new language.
4. Rule passion – faith - tradition and all things with tempered reason.
5. Protect people and nations with fair laws and just courts.
6. Let all nations rule internally resolving external disputes in a world court.

7. Avoid petty laws and useless officials.

8. Balance personal rights with social duties.

9. Prize truth – beauty – love – seeking harmony with the infinite.

10. Be not a cancer on the earth – Leave room for nature – Leave room for nature.

So as not to go too far off track the reader is invited to view Section 3 of "The THEorY of LIVEvolution" and the RC Christian page on my web site. In the latter Robert is associated with everything from the Egyptian gods Thoth and Osiris to the Greek god Hermes to the European Enlightenment to the French Revolution to Barack Obama/Barry Soetoro/whatever this guy's real name actually is. Also, Robert Christian ties directly to "The Order" as thoroughly documented by yours truly (see the **322, the eco wackos and the Georgia Guidestones** link on the bottom of the new age page).

In summary, Robert Christian slips in and out of history like a certain serpent in the Bible and no slouch in this 'game' known as Operation Genocide.

Getting back, that "Gaia Hypothesis" concept of limiting "Mother Earth" to one billion people (which is common for these wackos as per 'Operation Genocide', also see Their Lists page) brings to mind Anti-10 Commandment number one courtesy my new friend, our new friend, Robert Christian:

1. Maintain humanity under 500,000,000 in perpetual balance with nature.

Of course James Lovelock is slightly more compassionate than Robert by claiming "Gaia" can support around one billion people. One of the ways to achieve this goal is to have abortion doctors, the real "death controllers" since no human means no death later on, would be to sterilize welfare recipients and implement "green abortions" as per current "science czar" John Holdren. And this just so happens to align with anti-10 Commandment number 2:

2. Guide reproduction wisely – improving fitness and diversity.

Continuing, here's an excerpt from Section 2 of "The THEorY of LIVEvolution" that documents that these wackos really do consider global warming a "spiritual issue" to protect "our Mother":

Take a look at this pledge called the "Personal Energy Ethics Pledge" for all those "concerned" about "global warming":
As a believer:

That human-caused global warming is a moral, ethical and spiritual issue affecting our survival;
That home energy use is a key component of overall energy use;
That reducing my fossil fuel-based home energy usage will lead to lower greenhouse gas emissions; and
That leaders on moral issues should lead by example;
I pledge to consume no more energy for my use in my residence than the average American household by March 21, 2008
(emphasis mine)

Spiritual? Spiritual? What the hell is this, pun intended, some kind of joke? This is about science, no? God doesn't exist. The evolutionists (covered next) have told us so. So the earth's some kind of godless spirit? Sounds like many of these clowns are really earth worshippers just like many of those "ancient" pagan religions…We'll revisit this issue in Section 3.
Stay Asleep. Obey. No Independent Thought. Submit. Watch TV. Don't Question Authority. Marry and Reproduce. Consume.
By the way, a certain ex Vice "President" and "Presidential" candidate who has no problem flying in his own jet to accept every kind of Hollywood award from people with their own share of private jets for his propaganda film refused to take this pledge on March 21, 2007 while testifying before the United States Senate and Environment and Public Works Committee hearings….
How Convenient.

As documented on the new age page of my web site (www. boxofsunglasses.com), the Club of Rome works hand in glove with the UN-dead. Here's literally page one from "Mankind at the Turning Point", a Club of Rome book published in 1974 (just can't get away from "The Club" can we?):

CHAPTER 1

Prologue: From Undifferentiated to Organic Growth

The World Has Cancer and the Cancer Is Man.
A. Gregg *

Suddenly—virtually overnight when measured on a historical scale—mankind finds itself confronted by a multitude of unprecedented crises: the population crisis, the environmental crisis, the world food crisis, the energy crisis, the raw material crisis, to name just a few. New crises appear while the old ones linger on with the effects spreading to every corner of the Earth until they appear in point of fact as global, worldwide, crises. Attempts at solving any one of these in isolation has proven to be temporary and at the expense of others; to ease the shortage of energy or raw materials by measures which worsen the condition of the environment means, actually, to solve nothing at all. Real solutions are apparently interdependent; collectively, the

---

* A. Gregg."A Medical Aspect of the Population Problem," *Science* 121 (1955), 681.

1

What needs to happen to cancer? It needs to be removed with help from our other friends at the aforementioned "Camp Cancer" and the rest of the UN-American Genocidal Complex. Speaking of cancer here's literally anti-10 Commandment number 10 courtesy of the aforementioned Georgia Guidestones and our new friend (and leading candidate for "the spirit of anti-Christ") Robert Christian:

10. Be not a cancer on the earth – Leave room for nature – Leave room for nature.

Our new friend Robert Christian is covered extensively on "his" own section of my web page in addition to being thoroughly covered in Section 3 of "The THEorY of LIVEvolution". (See also the new age page on the web site). On the RC Christian page "he" serves as the inspiration to the Church of Satan/modern environmentalism, Saint John's the Divine Cathedral, MYSTERY, BABYLON USA or New York City. (The cap less pyramid atop Satan umm Saint John's is found on the front cover of my book "The THEorY of LIVEvolution"). Speaking of MYSTERY, BABYLON one should note in the Book of Revelation it is occupied spiritually by the whore of Babylon and interestingly enough Isis/Gaia/Mother Earth is also known as the "Mistress of the Pyramids".

Let's leave the church of Satan umm Saint John's and drive across town to the UN-dead where we'll find yet another religious environmental movement NGO or non-governmental organization (kind of like the IRS is "non-governmental") known as the United Nations Environment Project or UNEP. It was founded in part by the "Canadian Al Gore", an oil billionaire hypocrite by the name of Maurice Strong (who, along with Al Gore, has given sermons at Satan umm Saint John's the Divine). It describes itself as "fairly powerless" but look at its concepts right out of something subtitled with a term we should all be familiar with right now, "Sustainable Development". That title is, "Opinions and insights from the International Institute for Sustainable Development":

We require an Environmental Bretton Woods for the 21st Century...
The environment should compete with religion as the only compelling, value-based narrative available to humanity...

Now go back and read Robert Christian's Anti-10 Commandments again. Do they not describe this Operation Genocide mindset to a 'T'.

These UNEP nut jobs should hook up with the Club of Rome Gaia/ Mother Earth/Isis gang and they'll realize that "environment" is beyond "compete" and outright religion already. However, if "They" hang out at the core of the UN-American Genocidal Complex known as the United Nations "They" already partake in 'Operation Genocide'.

Let's look at one more excerpt from UNEP's "Opinions and insights from the International Institute for Sustainable Development". Check this one out in light of the current climate change/global warming/global cooling East Anglia University email scam that erupted in November 2009 like a volcano (natural disasters that dwarf any human influence on "climate change"):

As one member of the group expressed it: economics has great theory but lousy data while environment has great data but lousy theory. It is essential that the new UNEP narrative develop a robust theory to match its strong evidence of environmental degradation and its threat to prosperity, stability and equity. (40)

"Great data"? From these ***holes? They can't even decide if it's "warming" or "cooling" or ...never mind. Again, you're not dealing with rational people here.

Oh yes "The Wedding From Hell". It turns out that the order of the "Rose Cross" or "Rosy Cross" is another pseudonym for the Rosicrucian Order which in turn is another pseudonym for...Robert Christian. Now when Robert (who recall traces back to all kinds of "mythological" gods including the Egyptian Osiris and Greek Hermes) re-unites with "Mother Earth" (who remember traces back to Egyptian god Osiris' female half Isis or the Greek Gaia) it is considered "The Chymical Wedding". This marriage of the Rose (Robert) and the Cross (the four points of the cross representing the four kingdoms of nature earth, air, fire and water or Mother Earth) is also known as "The Age of Reason". This is where mankind 'reasons' with himself and decides he doesn't need God, the real One, and His pesky Rulebook. This Wedding from Hell is also known as "The Age of Aquarius" as in "this is the dawning of the age of aquarius, the age of aquarius, aquarius...yadayadayada...

So tell me what song did eco wacko high priest come out at the 2008 Democratic National Convention as he lap dogged for Barack Obama/ Barry Soetoro/whatever his name really is as the latter did his best Hermes/

Mercury impression as he spoke from between those idiotic Greek Temple 'decorations'?

Right, "The Age of Aquarius". Speaking of "*dawning* of the Age of Aquarius" have another looksy at Obama's/Mercury/Hermes campaign symbol again:

Image 3 removed (This image had to be removed for trademark issues; look at any Obama site at the "O" symbol that looks a lot like a rising sun)

And what else comes out of the UN-dead? The World A-hem Health Organization, part of the nucleus of the UN-American Genocidal Complex. But this is a more technical endeavor best left for Section IV. For now let's look at a company purchased by gang banker criminal JP Morgan back in 1895 and currently at the center of 'Operation Genocide' whose latest operation is mass starvation via corn based ethanol to solve the scam known as global warming/global cooling/climate change.

Speaking of JP Morgan, who was tight with "The Order", he just so happened to be the number one financier of the aforementioned Church of Satan and religious environmentalism, New York City's own Satan umm Saint John's the Divine Cathedral, cap less pyramid and all. Of course JP and friends formed another death-blow to "The Late Great USA" in the decades following Satan John's umm Saint John's Cathedral, the ongoing scam known as the "Federal" "Reserve".

Isn't this fun?

d. General Electric

In 1895 gang banker criminal mastermind JP Morgan purchased this leviathan of American industry. One of its operatives was a gentleman by the name of Owen Young who was right in the middle of the Dawes to Young Plans discussed before in Section II a. that essentially set up pre-war Germany for the second "war to end all wars". GE, like Rockefeller founded IG Farben, was a major cog in the wheel of the Nazi war machine. "Conspiracy theorist" Anthony Sutton tracks their nefarious deeds in his book "Wall Street and the Rise of Hitler". The following is from a chapter entitled "General Electric Funds Hitler":

That General Electric directors are to be found in each of these three distinct categories – i.e., the creation of Roosevelt's New Deal, the development of the Soviet Union and the rise of Hitlerism – suggests how elements of Big Business are keenly interested in the socialization of the world, for their own purposes and objectives, rather than the maintenance of the impartial market place in a free society. General Electric profited handsomely from Bolshevism, from Roosevelt's New Deal socialism, and, as we shall see below, from national socialism in Hitler's Germany. (41)

And who is tops on our Communist in Chief's White House Visitors Log? Why none other than Jeffery Immelt, CEO of the Nazi and Operation Genocide supporter known as General Electric....which brings me back to the focus of Section 3 of my first book, "The THEorY of LIVEvolution". There I discussed at length the religious home of the modern wacked out environmental movement, none other than the Cathedral of Saint John the Divine right here in New York City (and just discussed briefly here). The symbolism placed out in the wide open inside this church of Satan occupies most of Appendix A of "The THEorY of LIVEvolution" as well. Suffice it to say that it's nothing more than MYSTERY, BABYLON's (i.e., New York City's) very own Tower of Babel. It even has its very own cap less pyramid on top, symbolic of the ILLUMINATION of mankind's spiritual evolution to become God, the real One. (This cap less pyramid also happens to occupy the front cover of my book and the back of "your" "Federal" "Reserve" note).

The same cap less pyramid on The "Great" Seal with the ILLUMINATED eye of Osiris, another manifestation of the lie told by Lucifer way back in the Garden of Eden: "ye can be as gods"; the real goal of Adolf Hitler and his criminal overlords like General Electric. General Electric was created in the nineteenth century and taken over by JP Morgan and the Skull and Bones "Eastern Establishment" in 1895. Quite simply GE was controlled by the "They" of that time and is a big factor in the "They" of today.

In other words "They" were and are pursuing *spiritual* evolution, the *real* THEorY of LIVEvolution...just like Adolf Hitler and a certain couple in the original Garden of Eden.

And in order for the elites - whether it's Adolf Hitler or his supporting cast of criminal Wall Street gang bankers back here in "The Late Great USA" - to evolve spiritually "the imbecile majority" needs to be curtailed. This elimination of several billion "useless eaters" (to quote Rockefeller operative Hank Kissinger) and "cancer" (to quote our new friend Robert Christian along with the Club of Rome) need to be dealt with under 'Operation Genocide'. And of course you'll never hear anything like this on GE owned NBC or C(ircus)NBC will you? But with stupidity like NBC's "Green Week" you will get the propaganda cover for Operation Genocide currently known as "climate change". (Please note that this is not to disparage your run of the mill member of "the imbecile majority" that works for GE just like your run of the mill Freemason that may attend the local lodge but isn't in to outright devil worship like the upper ranks. But as "the conspiracy" comes on line these realities will become more and more apparent and people will have to choose "The Age of Man"/"globalism" or God, the real One).

From GE to Hitler to Operation Genocide this all comes out of the UN-American Genocidal Complex. Hey it only gets 'better'; how can we forget "Camp Cancer" and its ghoulish experiments like man-made cancer viruses? "Camp Cancer" is another component of 'Operation Genocide'.

Are you starting to get the feel for the extent of "the conspiracy"?

IV AIDS and the Doctors of Death

a. Basic Virology

This is a brief overview of viruses and the human defense mechanisms against them. Its main focus is to describe the tiny microbes of death known as viruses and what they 'should' do in nature.

Viruses are found in the world of microorganisms. Microorganisms are generally defined as single or multi-celled, independent organisms that can only be seen with a microscope. They are capable of self-reproduction and represent the lowest forms of life. Some are considered 'plants' like algae and others 'animal' like plankton. Bacteria are perhaps the most well known microorganism and fall in between 'animal' and 'plant' but still fit the definition of a microscopic, independent, self-replicating organism. Although many bacteria are pathogenic or disease causing some are 'good' including those that operate in sewage treatment plants to break down biological waste and return it to forms useable once again in nature. The key to microorganisms is self-replication; they contain the necessary ingredients to reproduce themselves: the genetic code of DNA, the protein synthesis (i.e., the very physical structure of the cell) of RNA, the enzymes to assist the necessary chemical reactions and mitochondria to provide the energy and so on. Again, they're independent; they don't need to live inside the human body or any other host to survive.

And then there are the viruses. These tiny packages of death elude an exact definition to this day; they don't really fit the definition of 'alive' but they get around and can't be called 'dead' either. They are essentially microbiologic parasites. Recall that microorganisms are essentially self sustaining because they contain all the 'ingredients' to both survive and reproduce. Viruses do not; they must invade a cell and use or 'steal' the host cell's raw materials to reproduce. Let's look at basic viral structure from the inside out:

1.Viruses contain either RNA or DNA as its 'genetic' material; never both. Hence viruses are classified as either DNA or RNA viruses and RNA viruses are further broken down in to negative and positive.

2.Viruses contain a limited number of enzymes to assist its own RNA or DNA to reproduce themselves. Whatever of these special proteins the virus doesn't have must be 'stolen' from the host cell that the virus is invading (not to mention the host's energy sources).

3.Whatever limited enzymes and genetic material (RNA or DNA) the virus has must be carried in a 'containment' structure. This 'containment' structure is made up of a protein coat known as a capsid. Some viruses have an envelope outside of the capsid with special 'spikes' or projected protein structures called glycoproteins.

Viruses don't even produce their own energy. They just 'float around' until they find the right host cell and then essentially invite themselves in. Let's give a basic overview of the viral 'life' cycle (remember while viruses are outside the host they're not really 'alive') utilizing the analogy of a common household burglar:

1. Free floating
Many will probably die off in this stage since they can't self-reproduce (or work for themselves). Essentially they must 'rob' someone else's 'house'.

2. Adsorption
The 'fortunate' virus finds an acceptable host cell and latches on (or a house that this micro-sized 'burglar' is capable of breaking in to). A low level burglar or simple virus will need a window at ground level while a high level burglar with more equipment won't fit through the window but will need to go through the roof and evade the alarm system. The 'targets' of these 'burglars' will be different also: an apartment or small house versus a large gated house or even a bank.

3. Penetration
The viral material including its DNA or RNA and enzymes are injected past the host cell's outer membrane into its cytoplasm. Essentially the 'burglar' virus uses its 'crowbar' or whatever to break the door, window or roof outside and is now inside the house.

4. Synthesis
The virus 'burglarizes' the host's materials for its own ends, to reproduce itself using the host's energy, enzymes, whatever it needs.

5. Release
Once the host cell's (i.e., the house or bank) materials have been pirated by the original virus to produce multiple copies of itself the host is no longer useful. It lyses or breaks releasing the now multiple viruses to individually start the process anew.

6. Cell Death
The end result of all this is that the host cell usually ends up dead (i.e., the 'house' has been emptied) while the 'burglar' viruses spread out and reproduce geometrically as this process keeps repeating itself with more and more viruses. Sickness or symptoms of this 'invasion' soon ensues as cells fall victims to this 'burglary' at a geometrically increasing rate.

God, the real One, gave us a wonderful, multi-layered defense mechanism against these invaders summarized as follows:

1. The Barrier

It starts with the outer barrier of the human body known as the skin. Viruses can't penetrate it, the parasitic 'creatures' must find their way inside via another route including open cuts, the nasal passage, oral cavities or the eyes.

2. The Innate System

This one is even more amazing. The virus 'burglars' that have gotten past the first line of defense must deal with this system that is made up of four basic parts: two different cells known as phagocytes (white blood cells) and natural killer cells, the complement proteins and the interferon.

Basically, the phagocytes and natural killer cells 'eat' a whole range of foreign particles that would include viruses. An invaded cell as a last resort to disrupt (i.e. interfere) the invader's attempt to 'burglarize' and reproduce itself releases a special protein known as interferon. Complement proteins are produced in the liver and they 'bind' to the surface of virus. In so doing they 'mark' the virus for destruction by the natural killer cells and phagocytes or they work to break open the virus outer coat (i.e., the capsid or envelope) thereby gutting the parasitic invader to death.

3. The Adaptive System

When the first two systems are overcome this third level system is called in to play. It consists of two general types of cells, B and T. This system needs to be activated when specific invaders like bacteria or virus has overwhelmed the first and second levels. B cells produce what are known as antibodies, special proteins that bind to an antigen, a molecule that the binding protein can attach (i.e., a glycoprrotein on a viral envelope). These antigen-antibody complexes work in several different modes including 'presenting' the virus to a natural killer cell. B cells have a 'memory' for producing antibodies to a specific invader. Even after an invader virus or bacteria has been defeated a remnant of B cells will remain that can immediately produce the correct antibodies to re-defeat the same invader. The other part of this system includes the T cells of which there are two types, Helper T cells and Killer T cells. Very simply, T cells are activated by another group of cells called dendritic cells. The dendritic cells and T cells 'meet' in the lymph glands whereupon the dendritic cells present the 'intelligence' on the viral (or other) invader that has breached the skin and overwhelmed the innate system. The helper T cells 'guide' the killer T cells as the latter literally eats up cells that are in the process of being 'burglarized' and ready to release a fresh batch of viruses. When all of the 'burglarized houses' (cells that have been invaded) are destroyed the invaders have been stopped.

It turns out that HIV-1, the virus that causes AIDS, specifically targets the helper T cells. This equates to putting a platoon of soldiers on to a battlefield with no commander and no plan on who to attack which essentially negates the immune response. In other words, it attacks the defense 'commander' specifically while at the same time it's a specific virus

71

known as a retrovirus that until recently has never been seen in human kind; more on this later.

There are a couple of key points to take from this basic background. First is the inherent stupidity of vaccines. By direct injection they essentially negate the first defensive wall, the skin. Continuing, they contain ready-made viruses (among other gross ingredients, see the **Swin(dl)e Flu** link on my web site). Granted these are called 'attenuated' or weakened viruses but they're viruses nonetheless. The theory is that these weakened viruses will elicit a B cell antibody response (recall from before that B cells have a 'memory'). While this sounds good in theory it doesn't make a lot of sense. First, many viruses including HIV and influenza are unstable meaning they mutate quickly and essentially appear as a 'new' invader to the bodies' defense mechanism. This is why a new flu vaccine is needed every year and HIV, which mutates even faster, will never see a vaccine it cannot defeat. Second, they're injecting live viruses directly into the host (i.e., the human body). While weakened there's no predicting what the unstable virus will do. If it doesn't 'behave' these 'attenuated' viruses can re-organize themselves into a more virulent offspring and they've just gotten a free ride past the skin courtesy the vaccine to do so! Thirdly, the vaccines contain all kinds of disgusting chemicals and preservatives including mercury, formaldehyde and detergents that make it look a lot more like raw sewage than anything that's beneficial in a human bloodstream. Continuing, by eliciting a false immune response they waste the body's natural limited resources in fighting a disease that may never show up. Finally, they may induce what is known as an autoimmune disease. This can occur if vaccine virus particles and other contaminants latch on to body organs that are then attacked by the bodies own defenses since the organs themselves are now seen as 'foreign'.

This whole scenario makes one wonder why "They" don't study the body's natural defense system to be as strong and as natural as possible so it's ready for any invader. Unfortunately, natural cures don't make billions for big pharmaceutical companies that can then 'polish' the shills in Congress and the overwhelmed and severely compromised Food and Drug Administration (FDA). Besides, vaccines serve as a convenient mode to stick unsuspecting sheep in the "imbecile majority" with all kinds of ghoulish real time experiments if not outright genocide. Don't worry there'll be more on this in the subsequent sections just in case you think this is overreaching.

For purposes of this book, the important characteristic of viruses is to realize that they are "host specific", they generally like specific animals (even bacteria aren't immune to these micro parasites) and specific cells within those animals. Experts in the field of microbiology refer to something called "the species barrier" and most acknowledge that it's very difficult for a virus to "jump species" unless they're 'forced' to in a laboratory setting like say "camp cancer". This is for two basic reasons. One is the outer virus coat be it a capsid or envelope can only bind to specific sites on a particular cell's outer membrane or wall. The other is that even if the virus enters its host the cell itself may not have the right 'materials' like enzymes available for the virus to re-produce itself. While viruses generally stick to their own this isn't always the case. Influenza type 'A' infects humans, swine and birds. But this has been the case for a long time; there has been plenty of time for viral/host interaction, particularly the agrarian economies of the Far East where birds, swine and humans are at much closer quarters and Influenza A is most prevalent.

And of course when the genocidal maniac gang banker Rockefeller led UN-American genocidal complex gets involved breaking "the species barrier" becomes a disturbingly common practice. "They" themselves have become gods with their new microbiology 'play sets'; 'play sets' that were developed in earnest with the American eugenics turned genetics movement and its former ally, "That Great Leader, Adolf Hitler".

b. Frankenstein Lives

With this basic understanding of viruses let's look at what the cancer virologists and others in microbiology related fields were up to at "Camp Cancer". Recall that "Camp Cancer" is none other than Cold Spring Harbor, the nexus of the original Hitlerites in the American eugenics movement that now is in the middle of the UN-American Genocidal Complex. Here's "conspiracy theorist" Doctor Alan Cantwell:

The cancer researchers coaxed all sorts of viruses into laboratory cell cultures. In addition, viruses were injected or fed into animals for the sole purpose of producing cancer, immunodeficiency, opportunistic infections, and a host of other fatal diseases.

New diseases were produced in animals by viruses that were forced to "jump" from one species to another. Scientists put chicken viruses into lab kidney cells. Baboon viruses were spliced into human cancer cells. Monkey viruses were grown in human blood cells. Ape leukemia viruses were inoculated into rat tissue cells. The combinations were endless. (42)

"Conspiracy theorist" and Doctor William Campbell Douglass employs satire at times to make his point of the potential dangers lurking when "the new shamans of medicine" start messing around with things that Nature (i.e., God, the real One) didn't really intend be messed around with. For example:

Around 1972 scientists developed a method for mixing genes at will from any two or more organisms on earth. *The genes of a duck can be mixed with the genes of an orange or a zebra. Thus far we haven't seen any quacking fruit or duck-billed zebras but it's not due to lack of effort by scientists playing God* (43, emphasis in original)

Doctor Douglass goes on to explain how plant genes can be inserted into the human genetic structure and even quips "...cabbage head may take on new meaning".

While these may sound funny it's anything but as he laments on the potential dangers of scientists playing God or just plain playing around with manipulation of earth's gene pool:

*With the advent of genetic manipulation, i.e., recombinant engineering,
some most incredible and deadly viruses can be manufactured with little
difficulty. One devastating possibility would be to combine the highly
contagious influenza virus with the genes of either the anthrax toxin, the
botulism toxin, or the toxin from plague. If this type of designer virus were
unleashed upon a population, infection of almost all of the populace would be
certain, especially in the cities, and death would very quickly follow. There
would be no treatment and diagnosis would be difficult.* This is not science
fiction. *This is today's reality.* (44, emphasis in original)

Mr. Douglass then goes on to describe some of the combinations
that have been tried: human females with monkeys, cobra venom and E.
coli (i.e., the bacteria found in the human digestive tract), cobra venom
with various viruses, etc. etc. One interesting genetic mix and match
involved SV-40 and E. coli (now Dr. Mary's Monkey from before becomes
one interesting primate). SV-40 is a virus inherent in Simian monkeys
that does little damage to its monkey host. But when passed in human
tissue cultures it "jumps species" and finds a new host, mankind, where
it causes cancer. Mr. Douglass documents a case where this type of
'experiment' was discussed at Andrew Carnegie's aforementioned "camp
cancer", the "spiritual" nexus of the modern American eugenics/genetics
effort according to "conspiracy theorist" Edwin Black. One of these
cases discussed included a case where Stanford scientists along with their
counterparts at "Camp Cancer" were ready to combine SV-40 (the monkey
virus that causes cancer in humans at the nexus of the aforementioned
"Doctor Mary's Monkey" fiasco) with e coli.

The good news is this particular experiment was shelved due to the
potential danger of producing cancer causing E. coli bacteria, the same
bacteria that live in your intestine. However, now for the bad news;
it wasn't long before something called "shotgun experimentation" was
developed. This is where the DNA of a particular microorganism are
chopped up and inserted into another. Mr. Douglass calls this "a form of
genetic Russian roulette". One possible combination would be E. coli and
malaria. Another possibility would be something like the current Swin(dl)
e flu, a 'mysterious' combination of bird, pig and human flu from three
different continents (more on this in the **Swindle Flu** link).

These real life nightmare scenarios being undertaken by the descendants
of the Adolf Hitler inspiring American eugenics movement at places like
Camp Cancer and its supportive universities and labs throughout "the

Late Great USA" is summed up best by two words from Mr. Campbell: "Frankenstein Lives".

Based on this it wouldn't be a big deal for some sheep and cow viruses to suddenly "jump species" and end up in the human gene pool. This "perfect storm" has manifested in the AIDS *family* of viruses. Ironically enough the AIDS *family* is a real cancer causing virus distributed by the Rockefeller elites behind the death merchants known as the World Health Organization to solve the human "cancer" of "Mother Earth" as per the globalist elites in the Club of Rome. Did you get all that?

Isn't this fun?

c. The Mysterious HIV (AIDS) Viruses

You may recall the story given by "the experts" in the early to mid eighties about AIDS. A green monkey bites some native and wham AIDS all over the heterosexual population in Africa that migrated over to Haiti and then to the United States where (somehow) it's no longer a heterosexual disease but now an exclusively gay disease. This was the official line anyway.

And "They" would never lie to us, right? Oh no this is the United States and we don't do genocide like that bad boy Adolf Hitler...

Even a layperson (such as myself) has to ask how a disease goes from a monkey giving heterosexual disease on one continent to an exclusive 'gay disease' in another, simultaneously. And how can "They" be so sure it's a "gay disease" when in Africa it certainly isn't? Already something doesn't add up. And based on the previous section on Virology this is highly unlikely; not impossible but rare. But when one realizes that the popular "AIDS" is actually a whole family of distinct animal viruses that all "jumped species" so suddenly the warning flags need to go up.

Let's start with naming the viruses in the class or family of "human retroviruses" specifically to clear up the confusion:

HTLV-I Human T-cell leukemia virus
HTLV-II Hairy cell leukemia virus
HTLV-III (original name) now HIV-1 (the 'common' AIDS virus)
HTLV-IV (original name) now HIV-2
HTLV-V (original name) still goes by this name

I put "human retroviruses" in quotes because prior to these five distinct animal viruses turned human microorganisms of death that turned up relatively suddenly in the decades of the 70s and 80s, there was never a case of an observed *human* retrovirus. So now we in the "imbecile majority" are being asked to believe that five of these things suddenly broke the "species barrier" in the span of 10 to 20 years after thousands of years of human-animal interaction. Let's concentrate on HIV-1. Please note from hereon I will use HIV-1 instead of the outdated HTLV-III or even AIDS. HIV-1 is the *causative virus*, Acquired Immune Deficiency Syndrome (AIDS) *is what it does*: it's acquired and then attacks the immune system which in turn leaves one open to all kinds of cancers like Kaposi Sarcoma and other diseases like pneumonia and turbucleosis.

Let's categorize why HIV-1 and its 'siblings' were an unnatural, manmade occurrence.

1. Animal retroviruses have never appeared in humans.

Retroviruses as a microbiologic entity were discovered in the early nineteenth century. Human retroviruses weren't discovered, i.e., they didn't exist until 1980 when they exploded on the scene with not just one but five distinct virus types. A retrovirus is so named because it works backwards or 'retro'. It contains an enzyme called reverse transcriptase which allows it splice the viral RNA in to the host cell DNA. Normally, DNA produces RNA which then produces proteins, the very essence of our physical being. In short, HIV-1 becomes part of the genetic structure fundamentally changing the cellular offspring into who knows what.

HTLV-1 is similar to a cow disease known as bovine leukemia virus (BLV), a retrovirus. HTLV-II is similar to a sheep disease known as visna virus, another retrovirus. If a virus has the same general characteristics such as molecular weight and appearance of another it's considered similar. HIV-1 was originally called HTLV-III with good reason, it 'looks' almost exactly like a combination of HTLV-I and II called bovine visna virus (BVV), another retrovirus. This isn't supposed to happen either, viruses "jumping" from cows to sheep and vice versa.

In summary, we have a *whole family* of novel human viruses that "jumped" from cows to sheep or vice versa and then "jumped" again to humans.

2. Monkeys, Green or Otherwise Don't Harbor or Transmit HIV-1

This I found most curious, and disturbing, in my research for an undergraduate class entitled Microbiology in regards to HIV-1 but the entire aforementioned family of new human retroviruses. None of the major science journals at the time including Lancet, Nature, Science and others ever claimed that HIV-1 came from green monkeys. In fact they were quite open in their analysis from where HIV-1 and its 'siblings' came from: sheep visna virus and bovine leukemia virus. Of course very few outside of the scientific community (and yours truly) bothered to read these very technically written journals. So the obvious question becomes why were all the experts openly discussing their findings which pointed to the cow and sheep origins of HIV and 'friends' yet nobody amongst this group went public and asked why or how this happened. And why were the leading "experts" at the time led by American scientist Robert Gallo, who was tied in with the aforementioned UN-American Genocidal Complex, telling the "imbecile majority" that some mysterious African Green Monkey was responsible for HIV-1 (never mind the other novel human retroviruses) when it was, quite simply, factually untrue?

This is simple, documented fact. "They" were blatantly lying to the "imbecile majority".

"Conspiracy theorist" and medical doctor William Campbell Douglass makes this very case with multiple realities (which Dr. Robert Strecker's "Strecker Memorandum" makes and that I personally corroborated in my own HIV/AIDS research paper in an undergraduate report for a course in microbiology). First, a case of a wild monkey biting somebody and transmitting HIV/AIDS has never been documented or established. Second, only *laboratory* held monkeys contain human HIV/AIDS like viruses; it has never been detected in green monkeys (or any monkey captured in the wild). Third, as per the previous section, the HIV/AIDS family of viruses mimics both isolated and various combinations of cow (bovine leukemia) and sheep (visna) viruses. Doctor Robert Gallo was at the forefront of the American effort to determine the origin and cure for HIV/AIDS in the 1980s. Dr. Campbell doesn't pull any punches here:

Where does that leave Gallo's monkey business? His monkey would have to be taken from Africa, inoculated at the Fort Detrick, Maryland laboratory (or similar sorcerers' workshop), and then taken back to Africa to bite a few million people – if monkeys transmitted AIDS to humans in the first place which they don't. (45)

3. The Genetics of HIV-1 Matches Cows and Sheep, not monkeys.

This one dovetails directly from the last reason. The science of genetics simply doesn't lie. The DNA of any living organism is sequenced or organized into triplicates of amino acid 'base pairs' called codons. This sequencing is very specific. When looking at it through a microscope, you can tell if the species is a cucumber or an elephant. Based on this, most if not all microbiologists were saying in the 1980s in magazines like "Science", "Nature" and "Lancet" that the genetics of the HIV (AIDS) viruses match those of cows and sheep. Dr. Campbell deems it "impossible" that the HIV (AIDS) family came from the African green monkey or any monkey for that matter. Here again is "conspiracy theorist" Doctor William Campbell Douglass:

Consequently, we know beyond a shadow of a doubt that the AIDS virus came from a combination of cattle and sheep and simply had to be a genetically engineered virus in a laboratory. Gallo knows this. Essex and Haseltine know this. How long will they be able to cover up the crime of the millennium? (46)

4. The epidemiology makes no sense

HIV and its human retrovirus siblings showed up around the late 1970s and there are several reasons why the epidemiology makes absolutely no sense; if it was natural that is. First, in Africa it was a heterosexual disease. Yet it erupted for all intents and purposes simultaneously right here in "the Late Great USA" as a "gay disease". In other words it specifically targeted young homosexual males in five specific cities including New York and Los Angeles. So one has to immediately put the thinking cap on and ask quite simply how relatively simple microorganisms such as HIV can be transmitted so differently in two separate places. There is no valid scientific answer to this very simple question; if it's natural that is.

Second, we've already discussed that human HIV outside of purposeful infection in American labs doesn't exist in any monkeys. Additionally, HIV in Africa started out in urban areas. If HIV was floating around in some mysterious monkeys it should have showed up first in the outlying areas and then migrated into the urban areas. In fact the opposite was true. Also along these lines HIV didn't start showing up in other parts of the world like Asia and Russia until a much later date. If it really originated in Africa these areas should have been infected at least as quickly as the US since African to Asia travel is at least as common as African to US travel.

Thirdly, the numbers don't add up. At the time HIV was discovered it was being tracked and its 'doubling time' was approximately 12 months. Remember, we in the "imbecile majority" were being told that a mysterious Green Monkey bit a native and voila "AIDS". Mathematically, this means that it would take this single mysterious native just under 20 years to reach one million of his or her unfortunate neighbors. However approximately 75 million cases of HIV showed up in African relatively simultaneously. One could argue that there were inaccuracies with the counting of HIV victims. However, if this were the case we would be left with an almost 'magical' virus that mutates and spreads like literal wildfire assuming the 'natural' Green monkey to native transmission. Any virologist or related scientist knows that for such a virus to mutate and spread that fast it would be a sure give away for an unnatural origin.

Fourth, during the initial time period of 1979-1981 in America HIV was considered a "gay plague" that exclusively attacked a group, homosexuals, in six specific cities:

New York, Los Angeles, San Francisco, Denver, Chicago and St. Louis. Doctor and author Alan Cantwell discusses this situation at length in his book "AIDS and the Doctors of Death". For example:

When AIDS became official in June 1981, the CDC was entrusted to see that the new disease would not become a serious problem in the United States. The agency assured "straight" America that there was little to worry about. After all, it was a "gay" disease.

IN JANUARY 1979, TWO MONTHS AFTER THE BEGINNING OF THE NEW YORK CITY HEPATITIS VACCINE TRIALS, THE FIRST CASE OF AIDS WAS DISCOVERED IN A YOUNG GAY MAN LIVING IN NEW YORK CITY. THE WESTERN VACCINE TRIALS BEGAN IN MARCH 1980 IN LA AND SAN FRANCISCO. SEVEN MONTHS LATER, THE FIRST CASES OF AIDS WERE DISCOVERED IN THOSE CITIES (47)

So one has to put on the "thinking cap" and ask how a virus magically "jumps species" in Africa affecting 75 million heterosexuals in central Africa and then magically shows up in gay mostly white males in six specific American cities simultaneously. Another guilty group was Haiti. But the Haitian government was steadfast in its claims that HIV came from America; not the other way around as many so-called "experts" were saying here. Somebody was being less than truthful.

The arguments can go on and on but when one steps back and looks at these simple facts something doesn't add up. But just to be sure yours truly isn't just pulling this stuff out of the air or my other sources are all crazy too, here are some excerpts from Lancet, one of the more popular scientific journals at the time:

Several independent lines of evidence now support the concept that AIDS is new in Africa.

There is no conclusive evidence that the AIDS virus originated in Africa, since the epidemic seemed to start at approximately the same time as in America and Europe.

The origin of HTLV-III/LAV is of more than historical interest. The AIDS agent, a complicated retrovirus with core proteins and a glycoprotein envelope, could not have originated de novo...the ancestor agent has not yet been identified.

Whatever the origin of the AIDS agent, it is now readily transmitted between human beings under certain conditions...in America and Europe...risk of infection being confined largely to particular risk groups such as homosexual men and persons exposed parenterally to infected blood and blood products. Transmission within Africa is less well understood but clearly it must be different from that in America and Europe since the sex distribution of African AIDS cases is nearly equal...(48)

"De novo" means out of nothing. In other words HIV didn't just show up out of thin air. This article was written in 1986 when "They" led by "experts" such as the aforementioned Doctor Robert Gallo of the National Cancer Institute (i.e., right in the middle of the UN-American genocidal complex) were so sure it came from African Green monkeys yet this article states "Transmission within Africa is less well understood..." as per the last sentence in this passage.

So one must ask how the "They" missed this one. It sounds like an exactly analogous situation to the "economic" experts who debate the "Fed" when in reality it's an obvious tool of economic ruination as "the Late Great USA" can never pay back the national debt.

Or for that matter, the "pristine bullet".

And, not coincidentally, the Rockefeller name, as usual, resides behind all.

d. WHO is Behind AIDS?

Another entity that finds a home at that depot of devil worshippers, eco wacko freaks and low life despots known as the UN-dead is the World a-hem Health Organization so one can see the problems starting already. This organization became the international clearing house for the study of all kinds of biological niceties like man-made viruses that were specifically designed to "jump species". Don't take my word for it; in the Appendix I present several pages from the WHO's own journal that document this macabre undertaking. So the WHO, at the center of the UN-dead American genocidal complex, was running around requesting HIV like viruses at the same time the eugenics to genetics types at "Camp Cancer" were doing the same. In 1969 the Army requested an HIV like virus. And WHO, no pun intended, was overseeing the UN-American Genocidal Complex at this time? That would be "Tricky Dick" and his Rockefeller operative (and today's recycled banksta criminal) Henry Kissinger. More direct proof of this is presented in the Appendix as well.

Just as documented in the **1984** link when it comes to the demise of "The Late Great USA" or if it comes from the UN-dead the genocidal maniac Rockefeller family and friends' fingerprints aren't far to be found. We've just discussed two prominent members of the UN-American Genocidal Complex, the WHO and the Department of Defense. It's said a picture is worth a thousand words and I've put today's UN-American Genocidal Complex into a summary graph. Some of this information was extracted from Dr. Leonard Horowitz's H1N1 Flu 2009 News Letter, Volume 1. In reality I've simplified it or else you would be looking at a plate of spaghetti but the point is made: "THEY", our devil worshipping overlords, do indeed "LIVE" (don't believe me? Check out the **Bohemian Grove** link when you're done here).

As per the previous section there's no valid natural reason for the mysterious HIV. The only vehicle that makes sense for the African origin of HIV is a smallpox vaccine that was widely distributed by the WHO in central Africa just prior to the disease's widespread breakout. This scenario was covered in a front page story of the London Times on May 11, 1987. However, it died quickly and no follow up was done. And of course the Rockefeller controlled corporate media kept any inkling of it from the "imbecile majority" here in "The Late Great USA". And as far as the homosexual community here the only pattern that makes sense for a new disease that targeted a specific population in six specific cities was the hepatitis B vaccine issued under the guidance of the UN-American Genocidal Complex . The vaccine trials were implemented by the blood bank in New York City and similar "free" health care facilities in five others (Chicago, Los Angeles, St. Louis, Denver and San Francisco). They were done under the auspices of the UN-American Genocidal Complex including the Centers for Disease Control (CDC) and the National Institute of Health (NIH) and a shady Soviet Doctor named Wolf Szmuness who ended up at another piece of the UN-American Genocidal Complex, Columbia University. UN-fortunately these types of experiments were (are?) commonplace amongst the "imbecile majority" courtesy of "our" Federal Government mostly through the UN-American Genocidal Complex. For example, approximately 1000 black males served as human guinea pigs in Tuskegee, Alabama to see how the disease syphilis progressed in a real life setting. The men were promised treatment but were actually given placebos so they were allowed to wither and die instead as they served as literal human guinea pigs. This is only the 'tip of the iceberg' for these ghoulish type of experiments courtesy "our" Federal Government. And, as usual, yours truly has the goods to shut-up the hot air windbags and other naysayers on both sides of the fake Hegelian dialect, the so-called FOX sNEWS "conservatives" and even more clueless "liberals". The Appendix includes some choice excerpts right out of a United States General Accounting Office Testimony entitled "Human Experimentation: An Overview on Cold War Era Programs". When you get there read the bit on page 4, "Chemical Tests and Experiments" that reads exactly like the American eugenics movement pre-World War II right through to this whole HIV/AIDS fiasco. And notice the verbiage on page 6 under "Biological Tests and Experiments", "…the Army conducted *several hundred* biological warfare tests in which unaware populations were sprayed with bacterial tracers or stimulants that the army *thought* were harmless." And the effects are widely unknown as the report admits "… possible adverse health effects related to the substances used were unknown or did not become apparent until years later."

How does that make you feel?

(Don't worry, I've provided some images so you can read this stuff for yourselves in the Appendix.)

But why? Why would "They" do this?

e. The Why?: "Ye shall be as gods"

It's quite simple actually. Perhaps many of the military and civilian scientists and other personnel don't really understand The UN-American Genocidal Complex, its sheer enormity, its utterly nefarious goals. Perhaps they thought they were doing the right thing by helping to prepare for the Soviet "evil empire". Maybe their intentions were noble but the results sure weren't (or aren't...AIDS is just the tip of the ice-berg...see the Swin(dl) e Flu Vaccine link on www.boxofsunglasses.com). "The road to hell is paved with good intentions" so the saying goes. How will God, the real One, judge these people or anyone else for that matter? I'm not Him, I certainly don't even pretend to know.

But for those in the know the answer to this question has more to do with the mentality exemplified in the radical or religious environmental movement. Given the rabid hatred of excessive population and even humanity itself by the wacked out eco wacko nature freaks the justification for unleashing such a nightmare is in place. I turn to Doctor Horowitz and his excellent book once again for an example of the mentality of these lunatics:

Some extremist U.S. ecologists go so far as to AIDS as a blessing. According to a letter from "Miss Ann Thropy" printed under an open letter policy in EarthFirst! Journal, "If radical environmentalists were to invent a disease to bring human population back to ecological sanity, it would probably be something like AIDS...We can see AIDS not as problem but a necessary solution..." (49)

One example of "extremist U.S. ecologists" would have to be EarthFirst! Whose website proudly proclaims "No Compromise in the Defense of MotherEarth" (see the logo in the Appendix). Interestingly enough in my first book, "The THEorY of LIVEvolution" I came across prominent "New" Age author Drunvalo Melchizedek via his book, "The Ancient Secret of the Flower of Life" (as in the Rose of the aforementioned Rosicrucians and "Wedding from Hell") where he confers with an "Ascended Master" by the name of Thoth, the ancient Egyptian god of wisdom (don't ask). Anyway, Drunvalo defended the United Nations' decision to deploy AIDS in Africa to help limit the world's population. So how many like him are out there? Former scientists and the like that come to these conclusions based on "contact" with "Ascended Masters"? Based on personal experience at the

United Nations' Lucis Trust and documented on my web site, much more than just him I'm afraid. Also recall in Section III "The Gaia Hypothesis" that states the earth is a living organism that cannot support more than a billion people. Another example of "extremist U.S. ecologists" would have to be the World Wildlife Fund (WWF) who boasts on its own web site about its first president, former SS officer Prince Bernhard of the Netherlands. The good prince (and ex-Nazi) also co-founded the Bilderberg Group with Rockefeller Family interests in 1954. (The Bilderberg Group is an annual gathering of international elites introduced in Section 2k of "The THEorY of LIVEvolution" and throughout my web site). What a shock we would find that Rockefeller name again in the middle of this whole mess not to mention its endless grants to eco wacko "useful idiots" like WWF (and of course you'll be hard pressed to find this information on WWF's web site).

Other criminal gang banker genocidal overlords that run in the same circles as the Rockefeller family including the Carnegie Endowment, George Soros, Bill Gates, Ted Turner and Warren Buffet are all too willing to provide the funding to these "useful idiots" to achieve what THEY really want: total worldwide control, political, economic, literal control of life and death. Essentially we have a two-tiered approach: Tier 1 is comprised of the eco wackos and low levels of the UN-American Genocidal Complex to spread the notion that de-population plans to save "Mother Earth" are justified. Tier 1 is sustained with ample funding from Tier 2, the Rockefeller/Skull and Bones death merchant overlords via entities like the Carnegie Endowment and Rockefeller Brothers Fund. In other words the Tier 1 "useful idiots" are merely clearing the decks and running interference thereby making the remaining population easier to control for Tier 2, our criminal master purveyors of death.

Maybe the cancer virologists working for the WHO and "camp cancer" thought they were doing the right thing by unleashing HIV and its cohorts; killing billions to save "Mother Earth". She's a goddess you know. After all if "evolution" is true then it doesn't really matter does it? Killing off a few million or billion "useless eaters"; what's the difference? If it is to save the rest of humanity and/or save "Mother Earth" it is all justified. Of course when a few million turns in to a few billion it's off to the races. This then is where Tier 1 has gone off track: by worshipping the creation (i.e., "Mother Earth) rather than the Creator, (i.e., God, the real One) as Paul laments in Romans 1:

Professing themselves to be wise, they became fools, 23 And changed the glory of the uncorruptible God into an image made like to corruptible man, and to birds, and fourfooted beasts, and creeping things. 24 Wherefore God also gave them up to uncleanness through the lusts of their own hearts, to dishonour their own bodies between themselves: 25 **Who changed the truth of God into a lie, and worshipped and served the creature more than the Creator, who is blessed for ever.** *Amen. 26 For this cause God gave them up unto vile affections: for even their women did change the natural use into that which is against nature: 27 And likewise also the men, leaving the natural use of the woman, burned in their lust one toward another; men with men working that which is unseemly, and receiving in themselves that recompence of their error which was meet. 28 And even as they did not like to retain God in their knowledge, God gave them over to a reprobate mind, to do those things which are not convenient; 29 Being filled with all unrighteousness, fornication, wickedness, covetousness, maliciousness; full of envy, murder, debate, deceit, malignity; whisperers, 30 Backbiters, haters of God, despiteful, proud, boasters, inventors of evil things, disobedient to parents, 31 Without understanding, covenantbreakers, without natural affection, implacable, unmerciful: 32 Who knowing the judgment of God, that they which commit such things are worthy of death, not only do the same, but have pleasure in them that do them.* (Verses 22-32, emphasis mine)

Notice the phrase where those that would worship "the creature more than the Creator". It is a concise summary of EarthFIrst!, the ex-Nazi Prince Bernhard founded WWF and the other Gaia nature freaks on 'Tier 1' of this "conspiracy". And knowing now where this kind of mentality leads perhaps you can see the point behind God's, the real One, out-right anger with these "fools", His word.

And Tier 2 goes off track when "They" try to become gods/rulers themselves. Then there's Lucifer, engine of the "New" Age. Adolf Hitler hero Helena Blavatsky readily admits this infatuation with Lucifer in her Magnus opus, "The Secret Doctrine". 'Lucifer' sits at the core of the UN-American Genocidal Complex as 'inspiration' to the UN-dead's Lucis Trust (if not the entire UN-dead itself). Here is what Lucifer told Adam and Eve in the Garden of Eden out of Genesis.

Now the serpent was more subtil than any beast of the field which the LORD God had made. And he said unto the woman, Yea, hath God said, Ye shall not eat of every tree of the garden? 2 And the woman said unto the serpent, We may eat of the fruit of the trees of the garden: 3 But of the fruit of the tree which is in the midst of the garden, God hath said, Ye shall not eat of it, neither shall ye touch it, lest ye die. 4 And the serpent said unto the woman, Ye shall not surely die: 5 For God doth know that in the day ye eat thereof, then your eyes shall be opened, and ye shall be as gods, knowing good and evil (Verses 3:1-5).

It seems "They" still want to take the serpent up on his offer and re-create heaven or the Garden of Eden right here on "The Late Great Planet Earth". Of course "heaven" could be greatly improved and easier to control with several billion less "useless eaters". And notice the passage about "your eyes shall be opened, and ye shall be as gods". Where does one see, no pun intended, the most prominent opened eye in today's society? Atop the "Great" Seal on the back of "your" "Federal" "Reserve" Note. Once again one can see, no pun intended, the true goal of "evolution": mankind's *spiritual* evolution or realization or ILLUMINATION that he can become God, the real One…minus a few billion "useless eaters", "morons", "misfits", "savages", "imbecile majority" and "Negroes" of course. And where does one see another cap less pyramid prominently displayed? Right on top of the modern day home of the religious environmental movement, Satan umm Saint John's the Divine Cathedral, New York City or MYSTERY, BABYLON USA.

Of course it's all good when it comes to the "…defense of Mother Earth" to quote EarthFirst!, on its own web site. It's beyond ironic that somehow *they're* not the genocidal maniacs, brainwashed lunatics and racists, people like yours truly are…according to them. That Lucifer or "angel of light" is good; no wonder God, the real One calls him "a liar and the father of them".

Go back and read history; it's littered with mankind self rule resulting in outright dictatorships of varying degrees of evil, Ancient Egypt, the Romans, the Catholic Church, Hitler, Mao, Stalin, etc. What makes the United States so special? Without God, the real One, nothing I will submit, just like our Founding Fathers warned. Murderous and megalomaniac dictators have always been around. This whole HIV/AIDS and "climate change" genocide fiasco with its religious environmental underpinnings is merely the latest, and most likely last, attempt to that end as God, the real One, laments in Ecclastises:

The thing that hath been, it is that which shall be; and that which is done is that which shall be done: and there is no new thing under the sun. 10 Is there any thing whereof it may be said, See, this is new? it hath been already of old time, which was before us. (Verses 1:9-10)

In other words, sinful mankind has always been the same: there's no asinine Darwinian evolution, there's no spiritual evolution and there's certainly NO program whereupon man can become God, the real One and start determining who gets to live and die on "Mother Earth".

The following passage in "War Against the Weak" caught my ILLUMINATED eye of Osiris, the "Angel of Light" represented on the back of "your" "Federal" "Reserve" note:

Everything Galtonian eugenics hoped to accomplish with good matrimonial choices, American eugenicists preferred to achieve with draconian preventive measures designed to delete millions of potential citizens deemed unfit. **American eugenicists were convinced they could forcibly reshape humanity in their own image.** (50, emphasis mine)

I'm not sure Mr. Black sees the implications of what he just wrote. But it sounds just like this passage from Genesis by God, the real One:

And God said, **Let us make man in our image,** *after our likeness: and let them have dominion over the fish of the sea, and over the fowl of the air, and over the cattle, and over all the earth, and over every creeping thing that creepeth upon the earth. 27 So God created man in his own image, in the image of God created he him; male and female created he them.* (Verses 1:26-27)

And recall this passage from Genesis 3:

4 And the serpent said unto the woman, Ye shall not surely die: 5 For God doth know that in the day ye eat thereof, then your eyes shall be opened, and ye shall be as gods, knowing good and evil (Verses 4-5)

So that's it. A hundred years ago it was eugenics and racial hygiene and then genetics. Recall that today's "American eugenicists" have surfaced in the fields of genetic research not to mention The Hastings Center and Planned Parenthood. Today it's the 'science' of global warming/ global cooling/climate change that drives the need to cure "the population

89

problem". When "The serpent" says "ye shall be as gods", these people have literally taken him up on it by trying to save "god's" wife, the female whore goddess Isis who today's radical environmental movement knows as "Gaia". Recall The Wedding from Hell when the other sun of god, Robert Christian, is re-united with Gaia or "Mother Earth" it's "The Age of Aqarius"/ "Age of Reason" according to the "New" Age fools or the one world satanic slave state predicted by God, the real One, "in the latter times".

So WHO is behind the UN-dead and its NGOs such as Lucis Trust (originally Lucifer's Publishing Company) and the World Health Organization, AIDS, the radical environmental movement and Nazi-American eugenics and just about every evil of history?

"That old serpent, the devil".

So whether it's the Ancient Egyptian ruling/priest class, the despotic Catholic Church, Adolf Hitler and now "the Eastern Establishment" of Skull and Bones, when one peels away the layers of "the conspiracy" you end up back in the Garden of Eden just like the Bible says. It's a funny thing that much maligned and despised Book just keeps re-surfacing. And have no doubt, in the end this is an evil "They" chose for themselves.

To conclude, "They", the descendants of the original Babylonian and Egyptian ruling/religious class, have worn out the patience of God, the real One, by playing god themselves. And God, the real One, is almost done playing around. This "conspiracy kook" can simply come to no other conclusion.

Now let me tell you about our new friend Robert Christian; pleased to meet you hope you guess my name...

APPENDIX: "The Conspiracy" in Pictures

An HIV like virus to cause AIDS like problems in the human race is requested by the UN-dead's World a-hem Health Organization, a tool of the Hitler financiers and UN-dead founders Rockefeller family.

Images 4-6 removed

Although I see the WHO as part of the US taxpayer funded UN-dead and therefore part of the public domain this apparently isn't the case. Therefore, these images had to be removed due to copyright issues. However, they can be viewed on the following link for PubMedCentral *"the**PubMed Central (PMC)** is the U.S. National Institutes of Health (NIH) free digital archive of biomedical and life sciences journal literature."*: http://www.ncbi.nlm.nih.gov/pmc/issues/169484/

That is directly from the web browser and takes you right to the .pdf for your own viewing pleasure. For convenience, a brief description is in order. Image 4 is the cover and there you will see "Bulletin of The World Health Organization Vol. 47, No. 2, 1972, pp. 139-274" along with some official looking received stamps from "The National Library of Medicine". For convenience here are some excerpts from WHO Bulletin Volume 47 No 2 dated 1972 (images 5 and 6):

Virus-associated immunopathology: animal models and implications for human disease

This memorandum reviews recent developments in viral immumopathology, with special reference to animal model systems, and indicates the possible relevance of the new concepts and techniques for certain diseases of man.

Recall that viruses are host specific so why are "They" messing with something that Mother Nature (i.e., God, the real One), didn't intend? "Because this is science" the myriad of detractors would say to which I ask the reader, based on what he or she has learned here, what the following passages describe:

Recommendations
   (1) A systematic evaluation of the effects of viruses on immune function should be undertaken....
   (2) The effects of virus infection on different cell types (e.g.,

> *macrophages, T and B lymphocytes) should be studied in greater detail...*
>
> (3) *An attempt should be made to ascertain whether viruses can in fact exert selective effects on immune function, e.g., by depressing 7S versus 19S antibody, or by affecting T cell function as opposed to B cell function...*

And here's some more later on...

(8) A major effort should be made to elucidate the role of immune complexes in the pathogenesis of viral hepatitis in man.

(3) Attempts should be made to compare the in vitro and in vivo effects of antibody and complement on the lysis of virus-infected cells...

This is describing HIV/AIDS (Note the focus on "viral hepatitis" and the "gay plague" of the early 1980s discussed earlier). Recall the quoted report from Lancet earlier that states *"The AIDS agent, a complicated retrovirus with core proteins and a glycoprotein envelope, could not have originated de novo...the ancestor agent has not yet been identified."*

Still not convinced? The next images ARE "public domain"...

An HIV like virus to cause AIDS like problems in the human race is requested by yet another member of the UN-American Genocidal Complex, the Department of Defense (which is closely allied with the National Cancer Institute and the rest of the eugenics ummm genetics "Camp Cancer" crowd).

[The (two) following files were transcribed verbatim by DataSource from original copies of the documents]

DEPARTMENT OF DEFENSE
APPROPRIATIONS FOR 1970

HEARINGS

Before a

SUBCOMMITTEE OF THE

COMMITTEE ON APPROPRIATIONS
HOUSE OF REPRESENTATIVES

NINETY-FIRST CONGRESS

FIRST SESSION

SUBCOMMITTEE ON DEPARTMENT OF DEFENSE APPROPRIATIONS

GEORGE H. MAHON, Texas, Chairman

ROBERT L. F. SIKES, Florida
JAMIE L. WHITTEN, Mississippi
GEORGE W. ANDREWS, Alabama
DANIEL J. FLOOD, Pennsylvania
JOHN M. SLACK, West Virginia
JOSEPH P. ADDABBO, New York
FRANK E. EVANS, Colorado

GLENARD P. LIPSCOMB, California
WILLIAM E. MINSHALL, Ohio
JOHN J. RHODES, Arizona
GLENN R. DAVIS, Wisconsin

R.L. MICHAELS, RALPH PRESTON, JOHN GARRITY, PETER MURPHY, ROBERT NICHOLAS, AND ROBERT FOSTER, Staff Assistants

Temporarily assigned.   HB 15090

PART 6

Budget and Financial Management
Budget for Secretarial Activities
Chemical and Biological Warfare

Defense Installations and Procurement
Defense Intelligence Agency
Operation and Maintenance, Defense Agencies
Procurement, Defense Agencies
Safeguard Ballistic Missile Defense System
Testimony of Admiral Hyman G. Rickover
Testimony of Members of Congress and Other
Individuals and Organizations

Printed for the use of the Committee on Appropriations

U.S. GOVERNMENT PRINTING OFFICE

129 -- Tuesday, July 1, 1969
SYNTHETIC BIOLOGICAL AGENTS

There are two things about the biological agent field I would like to mention. One is the possibility of technological surprise. Molecular biology is a field that is advancing very rapidly and eminent biologists believe that within a period of 5 to 10 years it would be possible to produce a synthetic biological agent, an agent that does not naturally exist and for which no natural immunity could have been acquired.

Mr. SIKES. Are we doing any work in that field?

Dr. MacARTHUR. We are not.

MR. SIKES. Why not? Lack of money or lack of interest?

Mr. SIKES. Would you provide for our records information on what would be required, what the advantages of such a program would be, the time and the cost involved?

Dr. MacARTHUR. We will be very happy to.

(The information follows:)

The dramatic progress being made in the field of molecular biology led us to investigate the relevance of this field of science to biological warfare. A small group of experts considered this matter and provided the following observations:

1. All biological agents up to the present time are representatives of naturally occurring disease, and are thus known by scientists throughout the world. They are easily available to qualified scientists for research, either for offensive or defensive purposes.

2. Within the next 5 to 10 years, it would probably be possible to make a new infective microorganism which could differ in certain important aspects from any known disease-causing organisms. Most important of these is that it might be refractory to the immunological and therapeutic processes upon which we depend to maintain our relative freedom from infectious disease.

2

96

The man overseeing a large portion of the UN-American Genocidal Complex and right in the middle of the American/Nazi genetics to eugenics transition was Rockefeller operative Henry Kissinger. Here is National Security Memorandum 200 where Mr. Kissinger gets right in the middle of the UN-dead/Rockefeller funded (Tier 1) Gaia weirdoes pushed "Population Problem":

NATIONAL SECURITY COUNCIL
WASHINGTON, D.C. 20506

April 24, 1974

National Security Study Memorandum 200

TO: The Secretary of Defense
        The Secretary of Agriculture
        The Director of Central Intelligence
        The Deputy Secretary of State
        Administrator, Agency for International Development

SUBJECT: Implications of Worldwide Population Growth for U.S.
         Security and Overseas Interests

The President has directed a study of the impact of world population growth on U.S. security and overseas interests. The study should look forward at least until the year 2000, and use several alternative reasonable projections of population growth.

In terms of each projection, the study should assess:

- the corresponding pace of development, especially in poorer countries;

- the demand for US exports, especially of food, and the trade problems the US may face arising from competition for resources; and

- the likelihood that population growth or imbalances will produce disruptive foreign policies and international instability.

The study should focus on the international political and economic implications of population growth rather than its ecological, sociological or other aspects.

The study would then offer possible courses of action for the United States in dealing with population matters abroad, particularly in developing countries, with special attention to these questions:

- What, if any, new initiatives by the United States are needed to focus international attention on the population problem?

- Can technological innovations or development reduce growth or ameliorate its effects?

- Could the United States improve its assistance in the population field and if so, in what form and through which agencies -- bilateral, multilateral, private?

The study should take into account the President's concern that population policy is a human concern intimately related to the dignity of the individual and the objective of the United States is to work closely with others, rather than seek to impose our views on others.

The President has directed that the study be accomplished by the NSC Under Secretaries Committee. The Chairman, Under Secretaries Committee, is requested to forward the study together with the Committee's action recommendations no later than May 29, 1974 for consideration by the President.

HENRY A. KISSINGER

Speaking of "Gaia" worshipping "useful idiots" this is right off of the EarthFirst! web site as it defends the Egyptian whore goddess Isis (or Gaia or Mother Earth) against her "cancer":

Image 10 removed

(This image had to be removed due to trademark issues but picture a large fist underneath the words "No Compromise in the Defense of Mother Earth" or simply visit the EarthFirst! web site and see it for yourself.)

Here are excerpts from 'your' Federal Government's Accounting Office 1994 Report discussing the aforementioned human experiments shenanigans carried out by Rockefeller-CIA-Nazi Paperclip UN-American Genocidal Complex types. Enjoy:

United States General Accounting Office

GAO

Testimony

Before the Legislation and National Security Subcommittee,
Committee on Government Operations, House of
Representatives

For Release on Delivery
Expected at
10:00 a.m. EST
Wednesday
September 28, 1994

Human Experimentation

An Overview on Cold War Era Programs

Statement of Frank C. Conahan, Assistant Comptroller General,
National Security and International Affairs Division

C6/080/15'2601

GAO/T-NSIAD-94-266

RESULTS IN BRIEF

During World War II and the Cold War era, DOD and other national
security agencies conducted or sponsored extensive radiological,
chemical, and biological research programs. Precise information on
the number of tests, experiments, and participants is not
available, and the exact numbers may never be known. However, we
have identified hundreds of radiological, chemical, and biological
tests and experiments in which hundreds of thousands of people were
used as test subjects. These tests and experiments often involved
hazardous substances such as radiation, blister and nerve agents,
biological agents, and lysergic acid diethylamide (LSD). In some
cases, basic safeguards to protect people were either not in place
or not followed. For example, some tests and experiments were
conducted in secret; others involved the use of people without
their knowledge or consent or their full knowledge of the risks
involved.

The effects of the tests and experiments are often difficult to
determine. Although some participants suffered immediate acute
injuries, and some died, in other cases adverse health problems
were not discovered until many years later--often 20 to 30 years or
longer.

Although military regulations in effect as early as 1953 generally
required that volunteers be informed of the nature and foreseeable
risks of the studies in which they participated, this did not
always occur. Some participants have testified that they were not
informed about the test risks. Government testing and
experimentation with human subjects continues today because of its
importance to national security agencies. For example, the Army's
Medical Research Institute for Infectious Disease uses volunteers
in its tests of new vaccines for malaria, hepatitis, and other
exotic diseases. Since 1974, federal regulations have become more
protective of research subjects and, in general, require (1) the
formation of institutional review boards and procedures and
(2) researchers to obtain informed consent from human subjects and
ensure that their participation is voluntary and based on knowledge
of the potential risks and benefits. We are in the process of
reviewing the effectiveness of these measures. A National
Institutes of Health official has stated that no mechanism exists
to ensure implementation of the key federal policies in this area.

2

THE GOVERNMENT HAS SPONSORED EXTENSIVE TESTING, BUT PRECISE INFORMATION ON TESTS AND PARTICIPANTS IS NOT AVAILABLE

Precise information on the scope and magnitude of government tests
and experiments involving human subjects is not available, and
exact numbers may never be known. However, our review of available
documentation and interviews with agency officials identified
hundreds of tests and experiments in which hundreds of thousands of
people were used as subjects. Some of these tests and experiments
involved the intentional exposure of people to hazardous substances
such as radiation, blister and nerve agents, biological agents,
LSD, and phencyclidine (PCP). These tests and experiments were
conducted to support weapon development programs, identify methods
to protect the health of military personnel against a variety of
diseases and combat conditions, and analyze U.S. defense
vulnerabilities. Healthy adults, children, psychiatric patients,
and prison inmates were used in these tests and experiments.

Ordering Information

The first copy of each GAO report and testimony is free. Additional copies are $2 each. Orders should be sent to the following address, accompanied by a check or money order made out to the Superintendent of Documents, when necessary. Orders for 100 or more copies to be mailed to a single address are discounted 25 percent.

Orders by mail:

U.S. General Accounting Office
P.O. Box 6015
Gaithersburg, MD 20884-6015

or visit:

Room 1100
700 4th St. NW (corner of 4th and G Sts. NW)
U.S. General Accounting Office
Washington, DC

Orders may also be placed by calling (202) 512-6000 or by using fax number (301) 258-4066.

Each day, GAO issues a list of newly available reports and testimony. To receive facsimile copies of the daily list or any list from the past 30 days, please call (301) 258-4097 using a touchtone phone. A recorded menu will provide information on how to obtain these lists.

PRINTED ON RECYCLED PAPER

Here's an example of the lap dog controlled press in lock step (goose step) with the American eugenics (and therefore Nazi eugenics) umm genetics racial hygiene push known as Health a-hem Care Reform right on time:

Image 16 removed

(This image, the front cover of Newsweek September 21, 2009 also had to be removed for trademark reasons. Picture a hanging plug with the words *"The Case for Killing Granny, Curbing Excessive End-of-Life Care is Good for America"* nearby. Of course the article points out the excessive costs of caring for the elderly but fails to mention the scam "Federal" "Reserve" system as this disgraceful rag lap dogs for "our" eugenics minded criminal masters of the UN-American Genocidal Complex. And on the bottom appears the George Will piece mentioned below).

Is this being too harsh? Just a couple quick 'fun facts': The young and old are worth less as per Population Council/Hasting Center (recall this is another Rockefeller founded disseminator of death) doorstop Doctor of Death Ezekiel Emanuel's "Complete Lives System". Also, Uncle Barry has taken "Science" czar's John Holdren's "green abortions" (the latest home of Margret Sanger's "Negro Project") to the extreme with his vote AGAINST the Born Alive Infant Abortion Protection Act. Umm that's known as outright murder...

One more thought. Notice Neo-Icon George Will holding his end of the bargain as the representative for the fake "conservative" right on the cover of this 'liberal biased' rag. This is right out of the Hegelian playbook of "The Order". (For elaboration of the Hegelian Dialect see the **Final** link on the Relevant News Page of my web site).

Here's a birds eye view of The UN-American Genocidal Complex with a reference from "Emerging Virus" Author Doctor Leonard Horowitz (fluscam.com) along with some additions by yours truly (more connections can be made but then it becomes a plate of spaghetti):

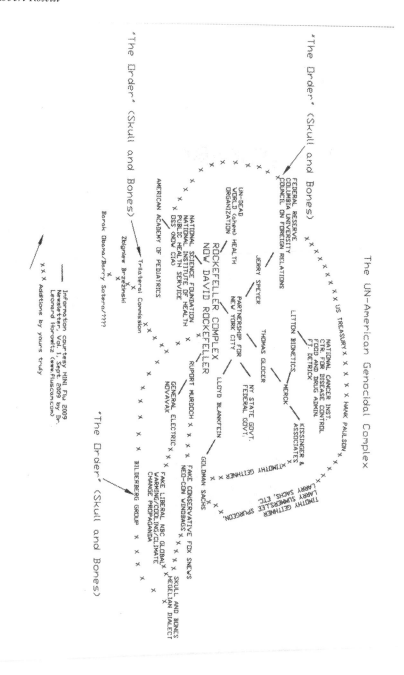

Notice that thing poking at the outside of The UN-American Genocidal Complex? "The Order" is presented by "conspiracy theorist" and author the late Anthony Sutton with the top additions by yours truly:

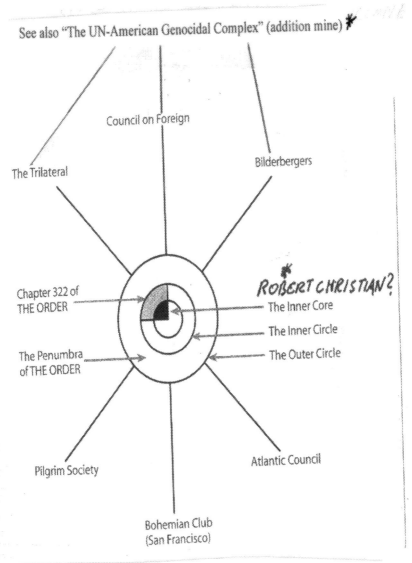

See also "The UN-American Genocidal Complex" (addition mine)

Council on Foreign

Bilderbergers

The Trilateral

Chapter 322 of THE ORDER

ROBERT CHRISTIAN?

The Inner Core

The Inner Circle

The Penumbra of THE ORDER

The Outer Circle

Pilgrim Society

Atlantic Council

Bohemian Club (San Francisco)

Main Illustration from "America's Secret Establishment: An Introduction to the Order of Skull and Bones" by Anthony Sutton.

And WHO, no pun intended, is at the core of "The Order"? Please allow me to introduce myself hope you guess my name. My new friend, our new friend, Robert Christian who pops in and out of history and acts just like the Enlightened god of this world represented by a certain all seeing ILLUMINATED eye on the back of "your" "Federal" "Reserve" Notes provided by yet another one of the pillars of the UN-American Genocidal Complex, "the Fed".

Isn't this fun?

Endnotes and Bibliography

1. Anthony Sutton, "Wall Street and the Rise of Hitler", (San Pedro, CA: GSG and Associates, 2002) back cover.
2. Ibid, p 31-32.
3. Carroll Quigley, "Tragedy and Hope: A History of the World In Our Time", (San Pedro, CA: GSG & Associates, 1966) p 308, 312.
4. Sutton, p 28.
5. Edwin Black, "Nazi Nexus: America's Corporate Connection to Hitler's Holocaust", (Washington, DC: Dialog Press, 2009) p 33.
6. Ibid, p 32.
7. Ibid, p 61
8. Ibid, p 48.
9. Margaret Sanger, Autobiography, (Mineola, NY: Dover Publications, 1971, 2004) p 374.
10. Margaret Sanger, "The Pivot of Civilization", (Middlesex, England: The Echo Library, 2006) p 28.
11. Ibid, p 33.
12. Angela Franks, "Margaret Sanger's Eugenic Legacy: Control of Female Fertility, (Jefferson, NC: McFarland and Company) p 43.
13. Dave Hunt, "A Woman Rides the Beast", (Eugene, OR: Harvest House Publishers, 1994) p 311-312.
14. Jim Marrs, "Rule by Secrecy", (New York City: Harpers Collins Publishing, 2000) p 36-37.

15. Doctor Leonard Horowitz, "Emerging Viruses: AIDS and Ebola, Nature, Accidental or Intentional?" (Rockport, MA: Tetrahedron, Inc 1996, 98) p 50.
16. Ibid, p 159.
17. Ibid, p 162.
18. Ibid, p 199.
19. William and Donald Scott, "AIDS: The Crime Beyond Belief" (Victoria, British Columbia: Trafford Publications 2007) p 298-299.
20. "Bilderberg Founder Prince Bernhard Tried to Overthrow Indonesian Government, Become Viceroy" infowars.com 12/9/09.
21. Edward Haslam, "Doctor Mary's Monkey", (Walterville, OR: Trineday 2007) front cover.
22. Ibid, p 187.
23. Ibid, p 277.
24. Doctor Leonard Horowitz, fluscam.com
25. Edwin Black, "War Against the Weak: Eugenics and America's Campaign to Create a Master Race" (New York City: Four Walls, Eight Windows, 2003) p87.
26. Ibid, p 411.
27. Ibid, p 411.
28. Ibid, 424-425.
29. Ibid, p 426.
30. Doctor Alan Cantwell, "AIDS and the Doctors of Death: An Inquiry Into the Origins of the AIDS Virus" (Los Angeles: Aries Rising Press 88, 95) p 71.
31. Ibid, p 70.
32. Ibid, p 38.
33. Anton Chaitkin, "The Nazi Euthanasia Program: Forerunner of Obama's Death Council", Executive Intelligence Review, June 19, 2009.
34. Paul Ehrlich, "The Population Bomb", (New York City: Ballantine Books, 1968) p 92.
35. Ibid, p 135.
36. Chaitkin.
37. Ibid.

38. Mihajlo Mesarovic and Eduar Pestel, "Mankind at the Turning Point: Second Report of The Club of Rome, (Bergenfield, NJ: New American Library 1974) p 127.

39. Global 2000 Report to the President Entering the 21st Century, (New York City: Penguin Books 1977) p 700.

40. United Nations Environment Project, "Opinions and insights from the International Institute for Sustainable Development".

41. Sutton, p 50.

42. Cantwell, p 38.

43. Doctor William Campbell Douglass, "AIDS: The End of Civilization", (New York City: A + B Books Publishers, 1989, 82) p 99.

44. Ibid, p 114.

45. Ibid, p 85.

46. Ibid, p 86-87.

47. Cantwell, p 82-83.

48. The Lancet, "The AIDS Problem in Africa", January 11, 1986.

49. Horowitz, "Emerging Viruses", p 180.

50. Black, "War Against the Weak", p 21.

Other Sources:

Alternet.org, "Government Experiments on U.S. Soldiers: Shocking Claims Come to Light in New Court Case", May 23, 2009.

Barren's Microbiology the Easy Way (Happauge, NY: Barron's Educational Services 2005).

Canadafreepress.com, "Agenda 21: The Death Knell of Liberty", October 12, 2009

Fightbackh1n1.com, "WHO memos explains how to turn vaccines in to a means of killing"

Marc Gladwin MD and Bill Trattler MD, "Clinical Microbiology made ridiculously simple", (Miami, FL: Med Master, Inc. 1995, 2008).

Dr. Stanley Monteith, RadioLiberty.com, "No One Calls It Genocide" DVD

Doctor Robert Strecker, "The Strecker Memorandum" video, 1990.

Lauren Sampayrac, "How Pathogenic Viruses Work", (Sudbury, MA: Jones and Bartlett Publications, 2002).